Android Tutorial Guide

A Step by Step Approach for Learning Android Development

Prepared by

Srinivas Mudunuri

Trademarks

Cover Design & Images By: Richard Castillo (http://www.digitizedchaos.com)

Printing History:

October 2015   First Print

ISBN-10: 1518761011

ISBN-13: 978-1518761010

Dedicated

To

My Mother
&
Son Abhishek

Table of Contents

Preface

This document provides a step-by-step approach for developing Android applications. It is specially designed to help the individuals who want to learn Android application development. This book can be used as a reference table guide for Android developers.

The Audience for this book is:

- Individuals who want to learn the Android application development.
- This book is primarily for beginners who want to learn Android application development.
- Individuals who are looking for step-by-step approach for developing Android applications.
- Individuals who want to learn material design components in Android.
- Individuals who want to learn location based services in Android.
- Individuals who want to learn open-source Android frameworks.
- Individuals who want to learn mobile database persistence frameworks.
- Individuals who want to learn Android studio for application development.

A prior knowledge of Java programming is required. If you don't know the Java, this book is not for you. It is good to have some XML knowledge but an XML novice can understand without much difficulty. Good have a prior knowledge of database programming. It is also good to have Java-Swing knowledge but it is not mandatory. This book is designed for beginners who want to learn Android application development. The chapters are arranged based on the increasing order of their complexity and its dependency. Inline code snippets are provided while explaining each topic and a complete working example is provided at the end of the each topic. A step-by-step approach is followed for developing code examples, so it is easy for a beginner to understand the application development.

The topics covered in this book are given below:

- Introduction to Android
- Activities, Intents, and Fragments
- My First Android Project
- Android Frameworks
- Android Material Design Components
- Android Database Frameworks
- Google Maps API - LBS
- Practice Project

This book covers the Android application development technology standards such as introduction to Android, Developing Android applications using material design components, Spring Android for accessing REST-based web services, Android location based services for to pin point the location on Google maps, Android open-source application development frameworks, how to use Android studio for developing Android applications, Android data persistence frameworks, the use of activities, intents, and fragments. A step-by-step approach is followed throughout and this book contains approximately 100 Java programs and images for a better understanding of the topics.

Structure of the Book

This book contains 8 chapters. The structure of the book is given below.

Chapter 1 (Introduction to Android) covers the introduction to Android application development, Android API version history, Android releases, Android software development kit, Android virtual devices, proxy configurations, anatomy android project structure, application manifest file, Android project files and folders, how to build and compile Android applications, and phone and wear emulators.

Chapter 2 (Activities, Intents, and Fragments) covers activity life cycle, various activity components, the need and purpose of intents, activity to activity communication using intents, fragments, activity and fragment life cycle.

Chapter 3 (My First Android Project) covers the commonly used user interface widgets, views, view groups, user interface layouts, develop your first Android project, creating menus and action bar components, creating list views, dialog spinners, using activities and intents, and creating user interface programmatically.

Chapter 4 (Android Frameworks) provide the details about open-source Android frameworks used in application development such as Spring Android, Dagger, Event Bus, and Picasso. This chapter also covers invoking the REST-based Web services using Spring Android, how invoke web services asynchronously, dependency injecting using dagger, XML parsing in Android, loading, caching, and transforming images using Picasso.

Chapter 5 (Android Material Design Components) will help you to understand the Google material design specification, Android material design widgets such as Material navigation drawer, developing material notifications for phones and wearable's, material colors, styles, themes, layouts, view shadows, and so forth, This chapter also covers the material animations, and material cards and recycler views.

Chapter 6 (Data Persistence in Android) will help you to understand the Android open-source data persistence frameworks such as SQLite, shared preferences object, Ream IO, and the JDK file IO. This chapter also covers the Android database operations such as select, insert, delete, and update statements, and so forth.

Chapter 7 (Google Maps API - LBS) provides the details of location based services, how to pin point the location on Google maps for a given latitude and longitude using Android maps API.

Chapter 8 (Practice Project) will help you to develop a practice project using material navigation drawer, material toolbar, fragments, activities, intents, themes, styles, material colors, and menus.

Tutorials – Code examples are provided for each topic. It will help you to develop the code; step-by-step instructions are provided for developing the code examples.

About the Author

Srinivas earned his master's degree in Machine Design Engineering from Roorkee-IIT, India. He is a Sun Certified Java Programmer (SCJP), Sun Certified Java Developer (SCJD), Sun Certified Enterprise Architect (SCEA), Sun Certified Business Component Developer (SCBCD), Sun Certified Developer for Java Web Services (SCDJWS), Bea Weblogic Certified Enterprise Developer and an Open Group Certified TOGAF-9 Practitioner. Srinivas has been working with

Java-EE related technologies since its very early days. He is a full stack Java-EE and Android developer. He has over 18 years of experience in developing the enterprise applications using Java-EE and Android technologies.

Srinivas is currently working as a senior Java-EE and Android developer in Phoenix, Arizona. He is an active member in various Java user forums and he is a regular speaker in Java and mobile user groups. Srinivas is a technology evangelist and he teaches Android, Spring, Web Services, and Java EE-related technologies during his free time. He is the author of following books.

- Imbibing Java Web Services – A Step by Step Approach for Learning Java Web Services.
- Spring Framework – A Step by Step Approach for Learning Spring Framework.
- MyBatis in Practice – A Step by Step Approach for Learning MyBatis Framework.
- Android Tutorial Guide – A Step by Step Approach for Learning Android Development.

Acknowledgements

This book could not have been written without the encouragements, supports and contributions from many people.

The primary references to this book are Java Specification Requests (JSR's), various Android articles, white papers, tutorials available on the web, my own experience with Java and Android application development. I would like to thank everyone who contributed to the Java and Android community which I used to gain the knowledge of Java and Android technologies.

First of all, I would like to thank my friend Uday Thota who helped me to build my career in USA. The sad part is he is no more with us; may Almighty God grant him eternal rest and may his soul rest in peace.

I would like to thank my friend Purna Katrapati; who helped me while doing master's thesis using C programming language and Surfer package. I would say he was my first teacher helped me to start my programming career. I would like to thank another friend Kishori Sharan; who trained me in Oracle and Power Builder technologies. This book would not have completed without Kishori's help and guidance. He is there to help me all the time, time after time and every time.

I would like to thank Richard Castillo who designed the cover page for this book.

I would like to thank my colleague Aziz Kadhi who helped me to learn Android. He shown me a path to learn the mobile application development and trained me in Android.

I would like thank my friends Rama Raju Saripella, Prabhakar Kandikonda, Gopi Krishnam Raju Sangaraju, Vijay Polasani, Madhava Rao, Ramesh masa, Raghavendra Swamy, Ravi Nallakukkala, Suresh Pattipati, Neeraj Oberai, Rakesh Jaiswal, Tej Kalidindi, Ranga Anne, Rama Chitirala, Madhan Retnaswamy, Ramesh Kondru, Bala Talagadadeevi, and Phani Tangirala. I would say simple thanks are not enough for their help and support. A special thanks to Madhan who helped me during my initial days of stay in Phoenix, Arizona.

I would like to thank all my students who provided me an opportunity to teach Java and Android technologies.

A special thanks to Sylburn Peterkin and Narayan Sithemsetti who helped me to review this book in spite of their busy schedules.

I would like to thank my childhood class mates Tulasi Narayana Rao, Venkata Appa Rao, Srinivas Baratam, Bhaskar Rao, and Siva Kumar. I have spent so much time with them and I do carry lot of childhood memories. Once in a while, I go to my home town they are always there to give a helping hand and warm reception.

Finally, I want to thank my wife Radha Mudunuri, my mother, father, brothers and in-laws who provide me great support and help all the time. I would like to thank my six year old son Aayush and three year old daughter Akshara; she has just started going to school and she always want to play with her cousin sister, Aakanksha.

Questions and Comments

Please direct all your questions and comments to mudunuri1234@yahoo.com

Source Code Repositories

https://github.com/mudunuri1234/AndroidBasics.git

https://github.com/mudunuri1234/AndoridLearning.git

https://github.com/mudunuri1234/AndroidNotifications.git

https://github.com/mudunuri1234/PracticeProject.git

Chapter 1. Introduction to Android

Android is a mobile operating system built on a modified version of Linux. Android is the most popular mobile operating system in the world. Android uses Java as its programming language for mobile application development. Android was originally developed in 2007 by a startup company named Android Inc. Later, Google took over both the company and the Android project. Google worked on several releases, making significant improvements in each. The first non-commercial version of Android (called Alpha) was released in 2007; the latest available Android release is called Marshmallow.

Android is an open-source project and is available for free under the Apache license. Many mobile manufacturer companies, such as Sony, Motorola, Samsung, and LG, make their own hardware using Android as the operating system for building mobile applications.

This chapter will discuss the following topics:

- Android fundamentals and architecture
- The history of Android, release names, and versions
- Android studio installation, set-up, and configuration
- Installing the required development tools
- Configuring proxy in your Android studio
- Creating your first Android project; understanding project structure, files, and folders
- The need and purpose of the application manifest file
- Configure Android virtual devices for phone and watch
- Using emulators to run the application
- Installing Android packages using the Android software development kit
- Using Gradle to build an Android project

Android Versions

The first non-commercial version of Android was released in 2007; many new features were added in each new release. The Android releases are named in alphabetical order. The following table provides the history of Android release name, API level, and release year.

Release Name	API Level	Year
Alpha	Non Commercial Version	2007
Beta	Non Commercial Version	2007
Cup Cake	3	2009
Donut	4	2009
Eclair	5, 6, 7	2009
Froyo	8	2010
Gingerbread	9, 10	2010
Honeycomb	11, 12, 13	2011
Ice Cream Sandwich	14, 15	2011
Jelly Bean	16, 17, 18	2012
Kit Kat	19, 20	2103
Lollipop	21, 22	2014

Architecture

The Android layering architecture is shown in Figure 1-1. The architecture has the following layers.

- Kernel layer
- Runtime layer
- Application framework layer
- Application layer

Figure 1-1: Various layers of an Android architecture

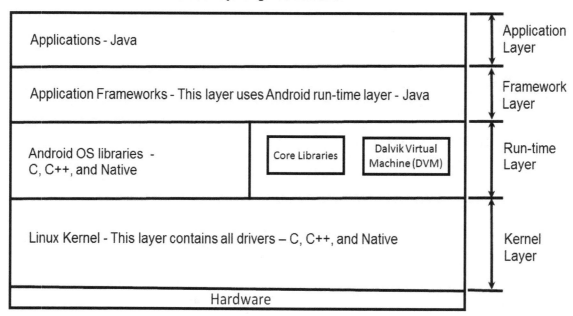

Android Layering Architecture

Kernel layer: This layer contains all drivers, such as the USB driver, keyboard driver, WiFi driver, mouse driver, audio driver, display driver, and so forth. These components are built using C, C++, and native code.

Runtime layer: This layer contains Android OS libraries, such as SQLite, Webkit, SSL, and so forth. SQLite is a lightweight data base for Android. Webkit provides browser functionality. SSL is used for security. This layer also contains the core libraries and the Dalvik Virtual Machine (DVM). Application developers can use core libraries to develop Android applications using the Java programming language. Dalvik is a specially designed virtual machine for the Android platform. Android applications are converted into Dalvik executables.

Application framework layer: This layer contains Android application frameworks such as package manager, view system, activity mangers, and so forth. Android OS platform capabilities accessed through application frameworks.

Application layer: This layer contains all user-created applications.

Development Tools and Technologies

The following tools and technologies are used in Android application development.

- Java Development Kit (JDK)
- Android Software Development Kit (SDK)
- Android Studio/Eclipse
- Gradle

To start with Android, download and install the JDK. The recommended versions are JDK 1.7 and above, so you can use the latest Java provided features.

Set the JAVA_HOHE environment variable.

Go to → Control panel → System and Security → System → Advanced systems settings → Select Advanced tab → Click on Environment Variables → Add new system variable JAVA_HOME = C:\JDK1.7.0   (This should be JDK's home directory on your machine)

Android Studio Installation and Set-up

Download the Android studio from Google's developer site. Figure 1-2 shows the latest Android studio available for download. An example Android studio installable file name is provided below.

android-studio-bundle-141.2288178-windows.exe

Install the Android studio with the default settings. The Gradle build tool is packaged with the latest Android studio, so you don't have to install it separately. After a successful installation, you will find the Android SDK root directory in the following location:

```
\Users\username\AppData\Local\Android\sdk
```

You can find the Gradle root directory in the following location.

```
\Program Files\Android\Android Studio\gradle\gradle-2.2.1
```

After successfully installing the Android studio, install the required tools and packages using the Android Software Development Kit (SDK) manager.

Figure 1-2: Android studio download site

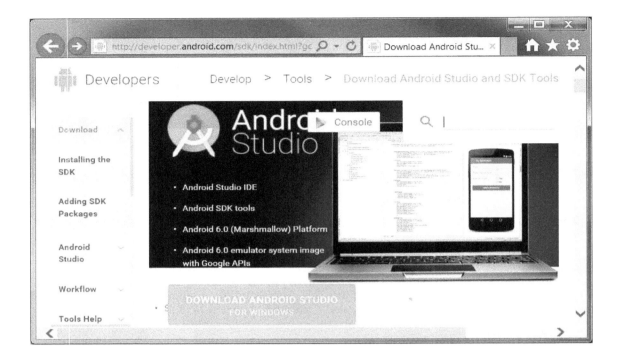

Android SDK Manager

SDK manager is used to install the required packages such as SDK tools, SDK platform tools, build tools, Android support repository, Web and USB drivers, play services, and so forth.

Open SDK Manager → Go to toolbar → Click on "SDK Manager" icon, as shown in Figure 1-3.

Figure 1-3: SDK manager icon

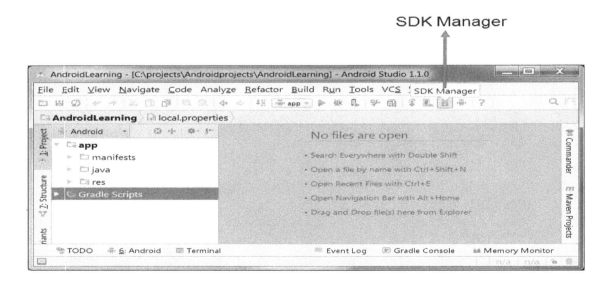

This will open a SDK manager window, as shown in Figure 1-4. Select the tools you want to install. Click the "Install Packages" button. This will install the required packages.

Figure 1-4: Android SDK manager window

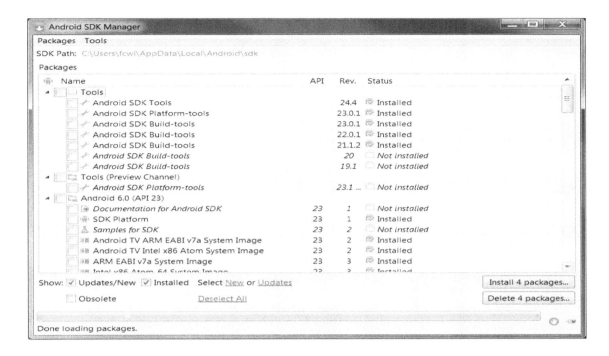

Install the required Extras → Scroll down to view the Extras, and install the required packages as shown in Figure 1-5.

Figure 1-5: Android SDK manager – Installing Extra packages

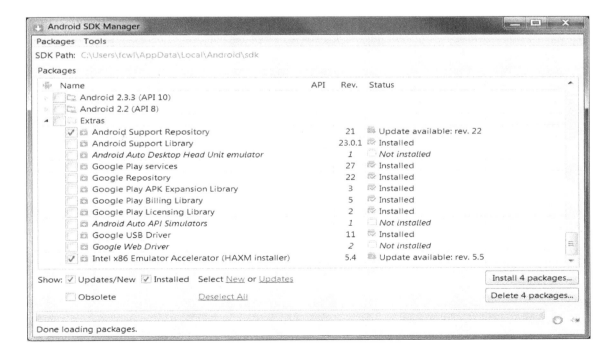

Creating Your First Android Project

To create your first Android project, follow the step-by-step instructions provided below.

Step 1: Open your Android studio. Go to File → New Project. Refer to Figure 1-6

Figure 1-6: Creating first Android project

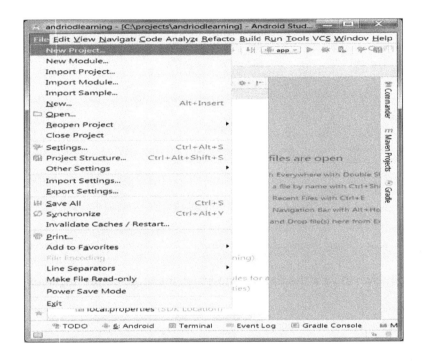

Step 2: Create new project window will be shown. Enter the details as shown in Figure 1-7

Figure 1-7: Configure new project

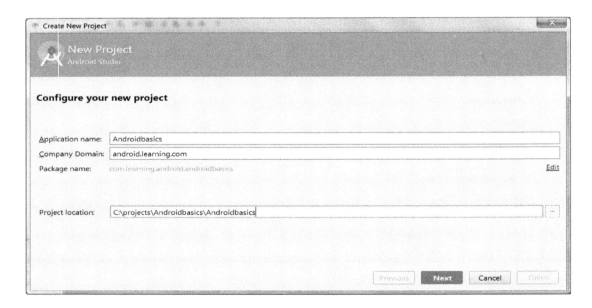

Step 3: The Activity window will appear. Select the blank activity. As shown in Figure 1-8.

Figure 1-8: Activity templates window - Select a blank activity

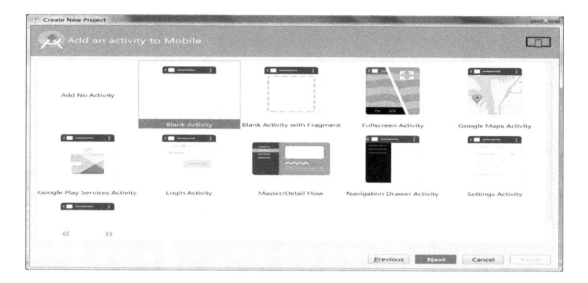

Step 4: The activity metadata window will appear. Leave the default names as shown in Figure 1-9.

Figure 1-9: Activity name window

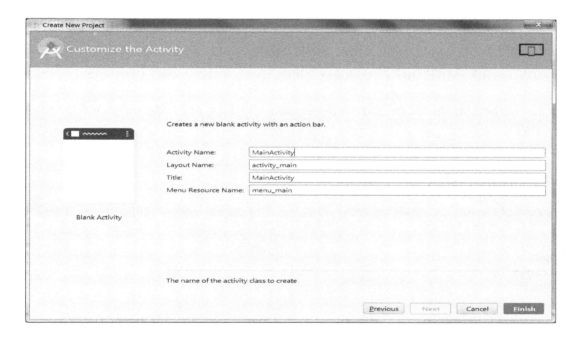

Step 5: Click on the Finish button. This will create a new project, as shown in Figure 1-10.

Figure 1-10: New project in Android studio

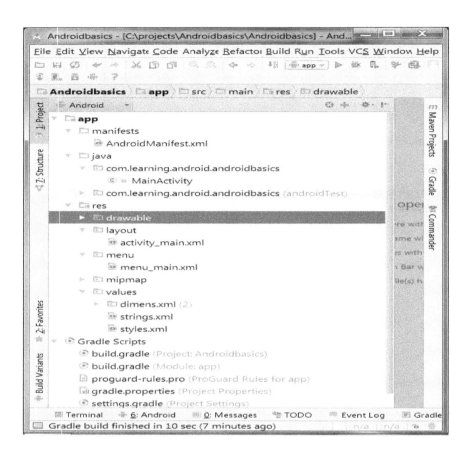

Anatomy of an Android Project – Structure, Files, and Folders

This section will help you to understand the project structure, files, and folders of your first Android project.

Project Structure, Files, and Folders

The structure of the Android project is provided below. The project explorer supports the following views:

1. Project
2. Packages
3. Android

We recommend you use the Android view, but you can switch to another view as needed. Figure 1-11 shows how to switch from one view to another.

Figure 1-11: Project Explorer in Android studio

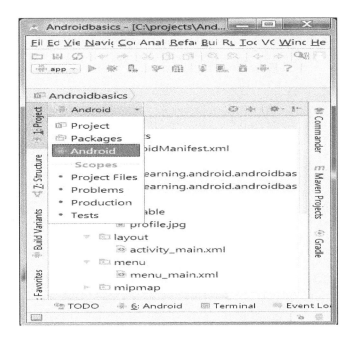

The following table shows the details about files and folders and how they are used in Android development.

File name	Significance
Application manifest file – AndroidManifest.xml	This file is available in the **"manifests"** directory. This file contains all your application activities, themes, and styles. All activity classes must be added to this file.
Java source files (.java files)	Create Java files and packages in the **"java"** directory.
Image files – ".jpeg" and ".png" files	Keep all images inside the **"res/drawable"** directory.
Layout files	The **"res/layout"** directory contains all application layout files. Layout files are used for building the user interface.
Menu files	The **"res/menu"** directory contains the toolbar, status bar, and navigation menus. The default created "menu_main.xml" menu file will be available inside this directory.
Static data files – labels and constant values	The **"res/values"** directory contains files to maintain the static data such as labels, styles, and so forth.
Build files – Gradle scripts	The **"Gradle scripts"** directory contains application build scripts. Add all your application dependencies (JAR files) to the "build.gradle" file.

Figure 1-12 shows the project structure, files, and folder details.

Figure 1-12: Android project files and folders

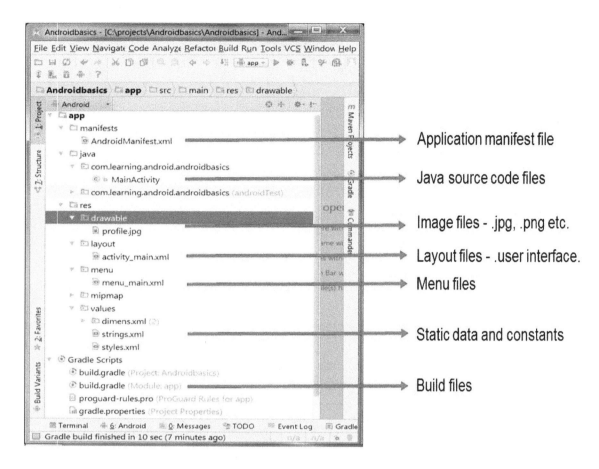

Coding Style and Notations

This section will help you get familiar with the code style and syntax. The following coding notations are used in Android application development.

The following code is used to access string resources from the "strings.xml" file.

```
android:text="@string/user_name"
```

The following code is used to declare a String array.

```
<string-array name="email_array">
    <item>Home</item>
    <item>Office</item>
    <item>Personnel</item>
    <item>Dummy</item>
</string-array>
```

The following code is used to access available image resources(.jpeg and .png) from the "drawable" directory.

```
android:src="@drawable/ic_launcher"
```

The following code is used to access declared themes and styles from the "styles.xml" file.

```
android:theme="@style/AppTheme"
```

Application Manifest File

Each Android application will have an application manifest file (ApplicationManifest.xml) in its root directory. This file contains the following information.

- Package name
- Main activity class which launches the application
- All dependent activity classes
- Themes and styles applied to the application
- Permissions required to access outside resources
- Application specific metadata

Figure 1-13 shows the structure of the application manifest file and its sub elements.

Figure 1-13: Application manifest file structure and its elements

```
<?xml version="1.0" encoding="utf-8"?>
<manifest xmlns:android="http://schemas.android.com/apk/res/android"
    package="com.learning.android.androidbasics" >         ──────────▶  Package name

<application  android:allowBackup="true"
     android:icon="@mipmap/ic_launcher"
     android:label="@string/app_name"
     android:theme="@style/AppTheme">                      ──────────▶  Theme name

  <activity
     android:name=".MainActivity"                          ──────────▶  Main Activity class
     android:label="@string/app_name" >
     <intent-filter>
        <action android:name="android.intent.action.MAIN" />
        <category android:name="android.intent.category.LAUNCHER" />
     </intent-filter>
  </activity>

  <activity android:name=".ProductActivity"/>              ──────────▶  Include other
 </application>                                                          Activity classes
</manifest>
```

Android Virtual Device (AVD) Manager

The AVD manger provides virtual devices to run your applications. These virtual devices emulate real devices. This section illustrates phone and watch emulator configurations. You can run your applications in the emulator; the physical device is not required.

Configuring Phone Emulator

Follow the step-by-step instructions shown below.

In Android studio, click on the AVD Manager Icon on the toolbar → AVD manager popup window will be displayed, as shown in Figure 1-14.

Figure 1-14: Create your emulator device using AVD manager

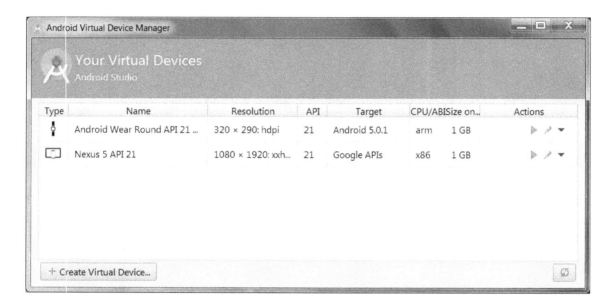

Click on the "Create Virtual Device" button. "Select hardware" screen will displayed, as shown in Figure 1-15.

Select "Phone," and choose the device name, e.g., Nexus 5

Figure 1-15: Phone emulator options

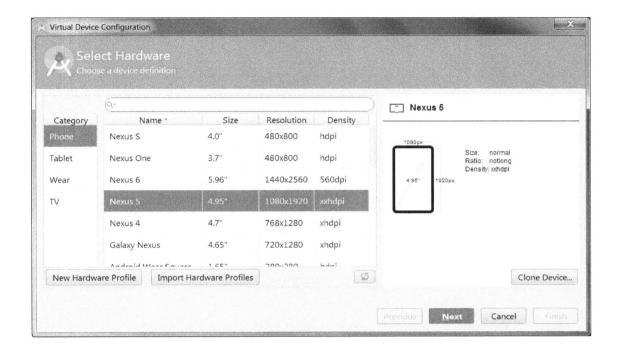

Click "Next." The following screen will be displayed as shown in Figure 1-16.

Select Release Name, e.g., Lollipop API Level 21.

You can install the required release from this window by click on the "Download" link.

Figure 1-16: Android API level options

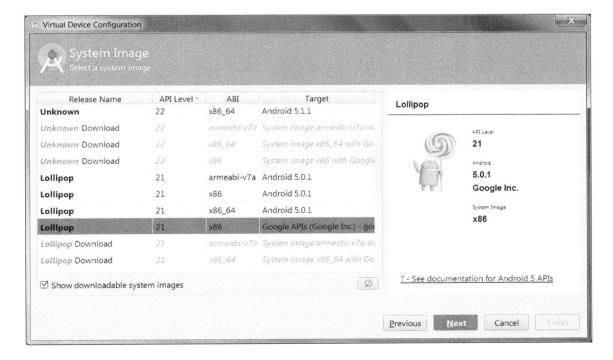

Click "Next", the following screen will be displayed as shown in Figure 1-17.

Figure 1-17: Advanced configuration settings for emulator

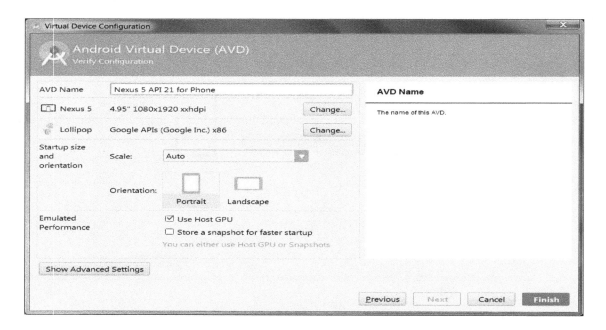

Click on "Show Advanced Settings." The following screen will be displayed as shown in Figure 1-18. You can update emulator settings such as orientation, RAM, VM heap, and so forth.

Enable keyboard input checkbox → This option is used to enable/disable the machine keyboard. By default, this function uses the emulator device board.

Figure 1-18: RAM and heap configurations

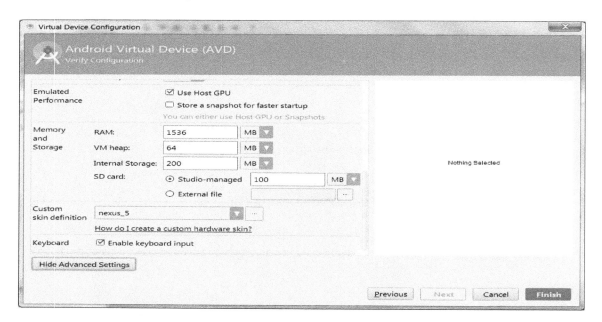

Click "Finish". The newly created virtual device is displayed as shown in Figure 1-14.

Run the emulator → Go to toolbar → Click on Run icon, as shown in Figure 1-19.

Figure 1-19: Android studio toolbar icons

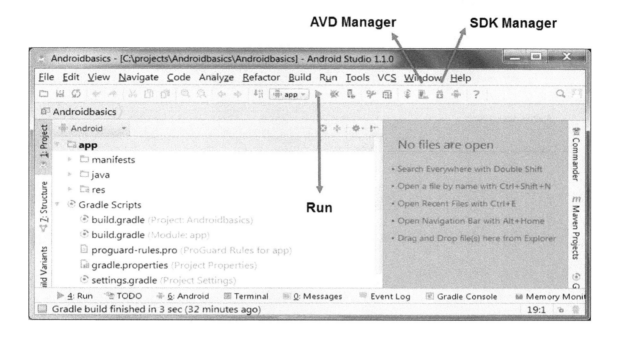

The following screen will be shown. Choose the previously created emulator device from the dropdown, as shown in Figure 1-20. Select AVD name → Click "OK." This will start the emulator.

Figure 1-20: Select emulator from drop down

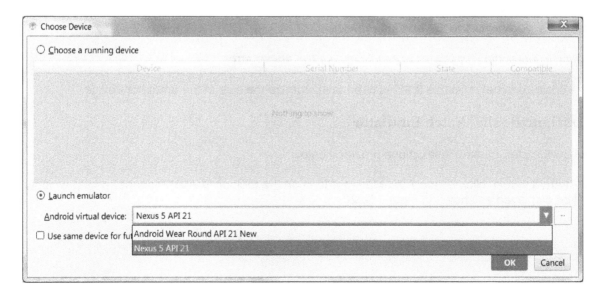

While starting the emulator, you may see the following error on console.

Emulator: emulator window was out of view and was recentered

FATAL:.//android/base/sockets/SocketWaiter.cpp:88:Check failed: isValidFd(fd). fd 1060 max1024

If you see this error, In Android studio → click on "Run" menu from toolbar → select "Edit configurations". The following screen will be displayed, as shown in Figure 1-21.

Figure 1-21: Emulator command line options

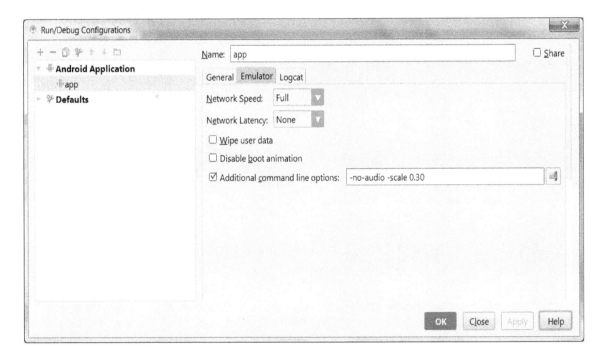

Click on Emulator tab → Select "Additional command line options." This field is used to pass additional parameters to the emulator device.

Enter → -no-audio. This parameter will resolve the above error.

The scale parameter (-scale 0.30) is used to customize the size of the emulator device.

Configuring the Watch Emulator

Follow the step-by-step instructions provided below.

In Android studio, click on the AVD Manager Icon on the toolbar → AVD manager popup window will be displayed as shown in Figure 1-22.

Figure 1-22: List of created AVD devices

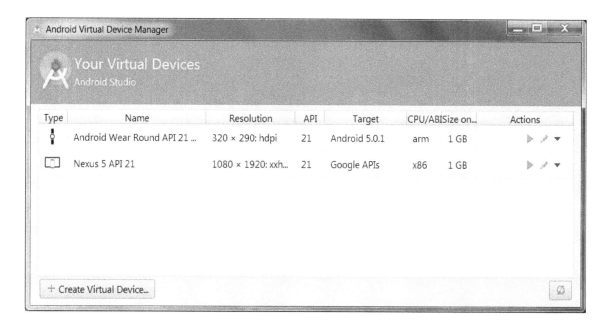

Click "Create Virtual Device." The "Select Hardware" screen will be displayed, as shown in Figure 1-23.

Select "Wear" and choose the device name, e.g., Android Wear Square/Android Wear Round.

Figure 1-23: Choose hardware device

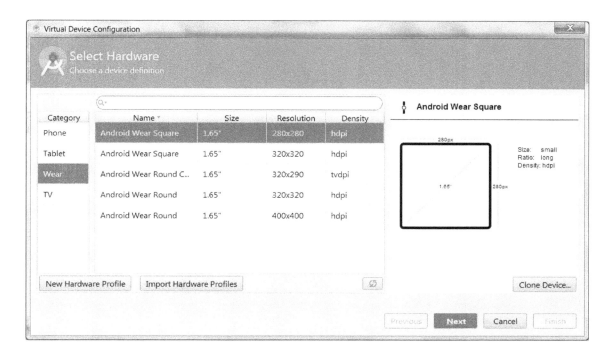

Click "Next." The following screen will be displayed as shown in Figure 1-24.

Select a Release Name, e.g., Lollipop API Level 21.

Figure 1-24: Choose API level

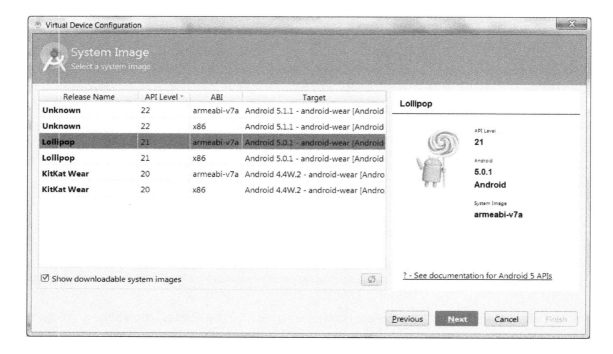

Click "Next." The following screen will be displayed, as shown in Figure 1-25.

Figure 1-25: Emulator advanced configuration settings

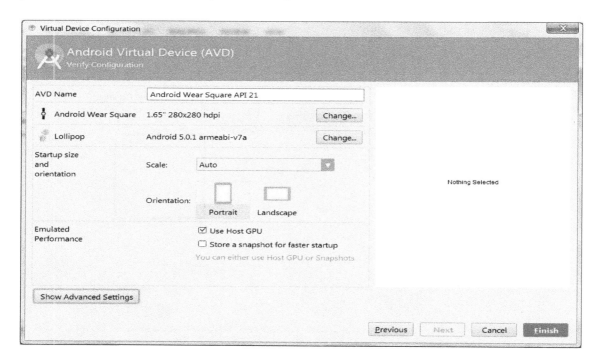

Click the "Show Advanced Settings" button. The following screen will be displayed, as shown in Figure 1-26. From here, you can update emulator settings such as orientation, RAM, VM heap, and so forth.

Figure 1-26: Emulator RAM, HEAP settings

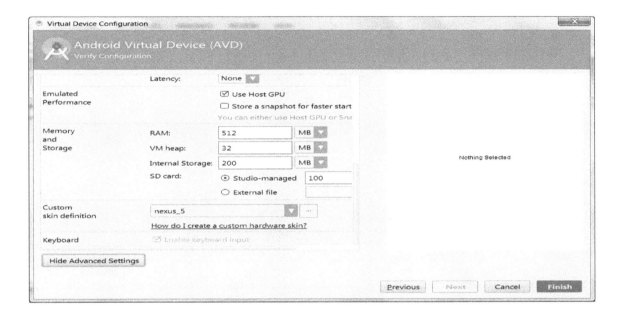

Click "Finish." The newly created virtual device is displayed as shown in Figure 1-22.

Run the wear emulator → Go to toolbar → Select "wear" from dropdown → Click on the Run icon, as shown in Figure 1-27.

Figure 1-27: Run icon on toolbar for wearable's

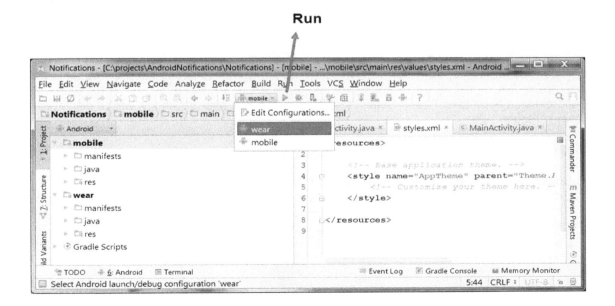

The following screen will be shown. Choose the previously created wear emulator device from the dropdown list, as shown in Figure 1-28. Select AVD name → Click "OK." This will start the watch emulator.

Figure 1-28: Selecting the watch emulator from drop down list

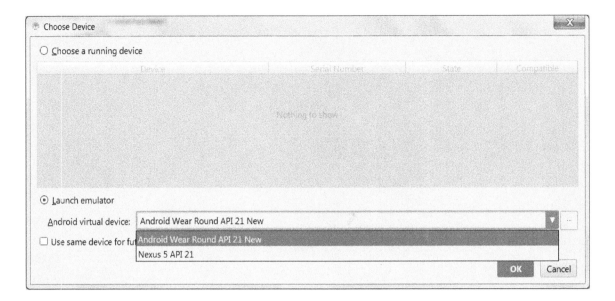

Proxy Settings

It is very common to use a firewall in a corporate company. Sometimes, you will have to pass through the proxy server to obtain authenticated access. In this scenario, you will have to configure the necessary proxy settings in your Android studio. If you don't have the firewall restrictions; these configurations are not required.

Proxy Settings for Gradle

Android uses Gradle to build the project. Gradle compiles the code, and downloads the required dependencies (JAR files) from internet. The following proxy configurations are required for Gradle.

In Android studio; go to → File → Settings → Select Gradle. A pop-up window will be displayed as shown in Figure 1-29.

Complete the following configurations.

- Select "Use default gradle wrapper" radio button
- Enter service directory path = your ".gradle" path, e.g., C:\Users\username\.gradle
- Enter Gradle VM options → -Dhttp.proxyHost=test.myproxy.org -Dhttp.proxyPort=8000 -Dhttp.proxyUser=username -Dhttp.proxyPassword=yourProxyPassword
- Click on "OK" to save the settings.

Figure 1-29: Proxy settings for Gradle

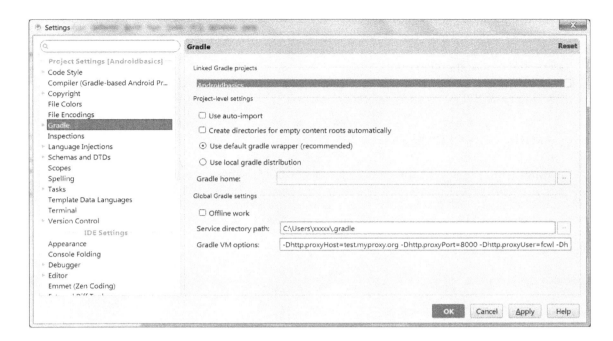

Proxy Settings for HTTP Proxy

The following proxy configurations are required for HTTP Proxy.

Figure 1-30: Proxy settings for HTTP Proxy

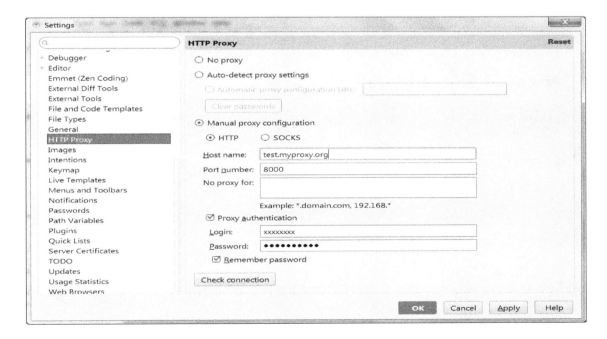

In Android studio; go to File → Settings → Select HTTP Proxy. A pop-up window will be displayed as shown in Figure 1-30.

Complete the following configurations.

- Select Manual proxy configuration → Select HTTP.
- Enter Host name = your proxy server name, e.g., test.myproxy.org.
- Enter port number → 8000 (your proxy port number).
- Select → Proxy Authentication.
- Enter login and password. Select "Remember password" checkbox.
- Click "Apply" and "OK" to save the configurations.

Proxy Settings for SDK Manager

The following proxy configurations are required for SDK Manager.

In Android studio, click on the SDK Manager Icon on the toolbar. The SDK Manager pop-up window will be shown. A pop-up window will be displayed as shown in Figure 1-31.

Enter Login = user name

Password = password

Leave the other fields blank. Click on "OK" button.

Figure 1-31: Proxy settings for SDK Manager

In the SDK Manager window, go to Tools → Options. A popup window will be displayed as shown in Figure 1-32.

Enter HTTP proxy server name = test.myproxt.org

Enter port = proxy server port = 8000.

Click "Close."

Figure 1-32: Proxy settings for SDK Manager – Tools - Options

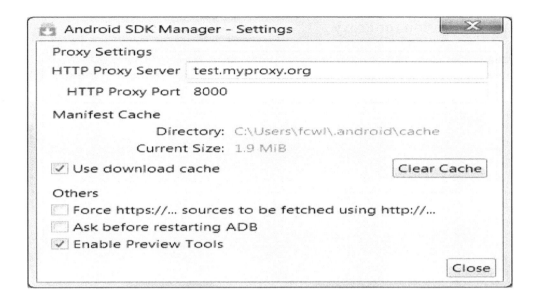

Proxy Settings for Compiler

The following proxy configurations are required for Compiler.

Figure 1-33: Proxy settings for Compiler

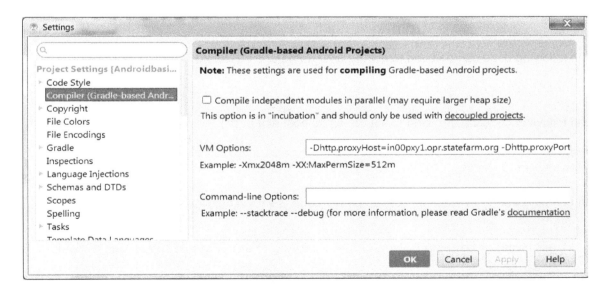

In Android studio, go to File → Settings → Select Compiler. A window will be displayed as shown in Figure 1-33.

Make sure the following compiler configurations are set.

- Verify VM options → -Dhttp.proxyHost=test.myproxy.org -Dhttp.proxyPort=8000 -Dhttp.proxyUser=username -Dhttp.proxyPassword=yourProxyPassword
- Click on "OK" to save the settings.

Using Java Authentication for Proxy

The following Java helper class can be used to obtain proxy authentication. Your proxy authenticator class must extend the `java.net.Authenticator` class. Listing 1-1 provides the proxy authenticator class code.

Listing 1-1: ProxyAuthenticator.java class.

```java
package com.example.andriodlearning.spring;

import java.net.Authenticator;
import java.net.PasswordAuthentication;

// ProxyAuthenticator.java
public class ProxyAuthenticator extends Authenticator {

    private String user, password;

    public ProxyAuthenticator(String user, String password) {
        this.user = user;
        this.password = password;
    }

    protected PasswordAuthentication getPasswordAuthentication() {
        return new PasswordAuthentication(user,
                    password.toCharArray());
    }
}
```

The following code can be used to set the user name and password.

```java
Authenticator.setDefault(new ProxyAuthenticator("username","pass"));
```

The following code can be used to set the proxy host and port.

```java
System.setProperty("http.proxyHost","test.myproxy.com");
System.setProperty("http.proxyPort", "8000");
```

An example use of Java authentication helper code is shown below.

```java
private Map<String, String> invokeRestService() {
    Authenticator.setDefault(new ProxyAuthenticator("username","pass"));
    System.setProperty("http.proxyHost","test.myproxy.com");
    System.setProperty("http.proxyPort", "8000");

    ...
}
```

Build, Run, and Edit Configurations

The most commonly used actions in Android studio are "Build" and "Run." Click on the Build menu from the toolbar; use "Clean Project" for cleaning the project. Use "Rebuild Project" to compile and rebuild the project. Figure 1-34 shows the available build options in Android studio.

Figure 1-34: Showing build options in Android studio

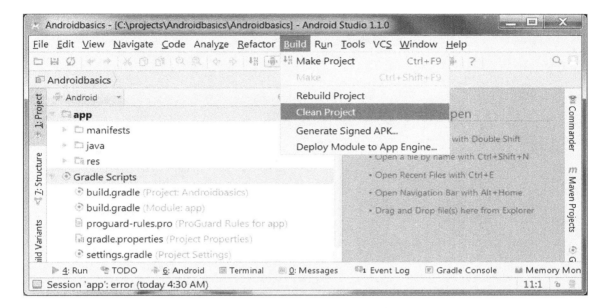

Figure 1-35: Showing Run options in Android studio

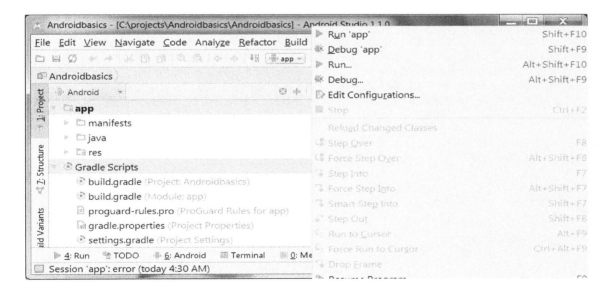

Similarly, Figure 1-35 shows the available "Run" options in Android studio. "Run" is used to run the application in the Android device or emulator.

Figure 1-36 shows the "Edit Configurations" screen. The screen is used pass additional command line parameters to the Android emulator.

Figure 1-36: Showing emulator command line options in Android studio

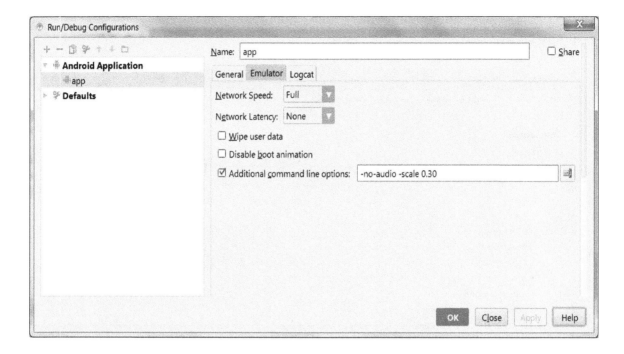

Using Gradle

Android uses Gradle to build and compile code. This file has the details of a compiled SDK version, minimum SDK version, target SDK version, and required JAR files for compilation. Gradle uses this data while compiling and building the application. All Gradle files are packaged inside the "Gradle Scripts" directory of your project. The name of your application build file is "build.gradle," and this file is created inside the "Gradle Scripts" directory. The "Gradle Scripts" directory structure is shown in Figure 1-37.

Figure 1-37: Showing Gradle build scripts in Android studio

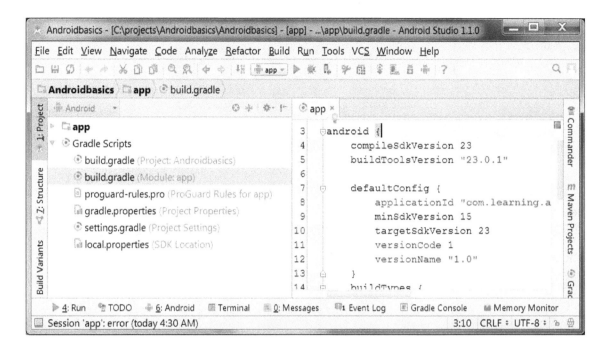

Open the "build.gradle" file inside your Android studio. An example "build.gradle" file is provided below. Note the inline comments in the code.

```
android {
    // Compiled SDK version
    compileSdkVersion 23

    // Build tools version
    buildToolsVersion "23.0.1"

    defaultConfig {
        applicationId "com.learning.android.androidbasics"

        // Minimum SDK version 15 is used; so
        // it supports the wide veriety of devices
        minSdkVersion 15

        // Target SDK version used = 23
        targetSdkVersion 23

        // Application code versions
        versionCode 1
        versionName "1.0"
    }

    buildTypes {
        release {
            minifyEnabled false
            proguardFiles getDefaultProguardFile(
            'proguard-android.txt'), 'proguard-rules.pro'
        }
```

```
    }
}

// Add all your dependencies here
dependencies {
    compile fileTree(dir: 'libs', include: ['*.jar'])

    // This "appcompat" version depends on buildToolsVersion
    compile 'com.android.support:appcompat-v7:23.0.1'

    // Example: Adding cards and recylerview dependencies
    compile 'com.android.support:recyclerview-v7:21.+'
    compile 'com.android.support:cardview-v7:21.+'
}
```

If you make any modifications to the application build "build.gradle" file, the Android studio shows a warning message that you must synchronize the project, as shown in Figure 1-38.

Click on "Sync Now" to compile the code.

Figure 1-38: Showing Gradle compile option in Android studio

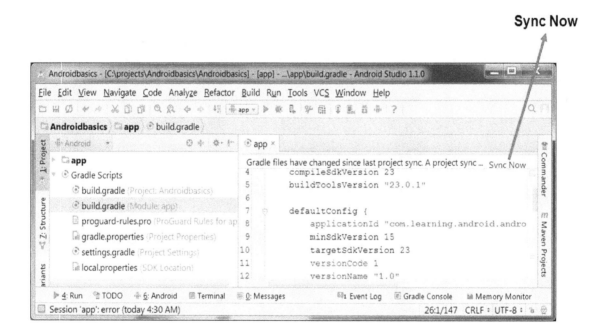

Design and Text View

In Android studio, you can view your layout files in either text or design format. The text view shows the layout code in XML format. The design view shows the user interface as it appears in the emulator device. Also, you can choose the type of device and API level at which to view the layout design. Figure 1-39 shows the design and text view of a layout file. By clicking on the design and text tabs, you can switch from design view to text view and vice-versa.

Design and Text View

Figure 1-39: Showing design and text view in Android studio

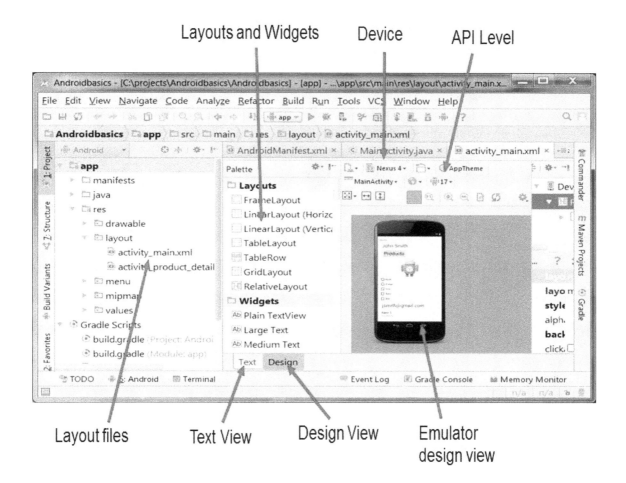

Summary

This section summarizes the Android fundamentals discussed in this chapter. Figure 1-40 summarizes the most important points described in this chapter.

- Android is a mobile operating system built on a modified version of Linux.
- The various layers of Android architecture are the kernel layer, run-time layer, application framework layer, and application layer.
- The SDK manager is used to install the required packages, such as SDK tools, SDK platform tools, build tools, Android support repository, Android support library, web and USB drivers, play services, and so forth.
- The AVD manger provides virtual devices to run your applications. These virtual devices emulate physical devices such as a phone or watch.
- Android SDK and the Java programming language are used in Android application development.
- Gradle is used to compile and build Android applications

Figure 1-40 Android fundaments

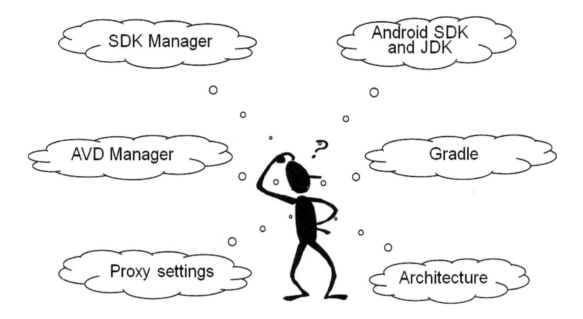

Chapter 2. Activities, Intents, and Fragments

This chapter illustrates the uses of various Android components such as Activities, Intents, Fragments, and so forth. These components are used in Android application development. Every Android developer must understand the use and purpose of these components.

This chapter will discuss the following topics:

- The life cycle of an activity class
- The life cycle of a fragment class
- The relation between activities and fragments
- The need and purpose of intents and how to use intents
- How to communicate between two activities

Activities

Activities are used to build the application user interface. The activity class renders the XML layout file. The activity class can access the user interface widgets defined in the layout XML file. An application can contain many activities; and they can communicate with each other in a loosely coupled manner. The following rules apply to an activity class.

An activity class must extend the `android.app.Activity` class. An example code is provided below.

```
public class MyFirstActivity extends Activity {
    ...
}
```

Add all your application activity classes to an application manifest file. An example code is provided below.

```
<?xml version="1.0" encoding="utf-8"?>
<manifest xmlns:android="http://schemas.android.com/apk/res/android"
    package="com.learning.android.androidbasics" >

    <application ...>
        <activity android:name=".ProductActivity"/>
        <activity android:name=".ProductDetailsActivity"/>
    </application>

</manifest>
```

The activity class `onCreate(...)` method renders the user interface layout. This is the first method called when an activity is created. An example code is provided below.

```
protected void onCreate(Bundle savedInstanceState) {
    super.onCreate(savedInstanceState);
    setContentView(R.layout.activity_main);
```

```
    . . .
}
```

The following code loads the XML layout `activity_main.xml` file.

```
setContentView(R.layout.activity_main);
```


Activity Life Cycle

Activity class has the following life cycle methods.

- onCreate()
- onStart()
- onResume()
- onPause()
- onStop()
- onDestroy()

onCreate(): This is the first method to be called when an activity is created. This method renders the layout XML file. See the example code below.

```
protected void onCreate(Bundle savedInstanceState) {
    super.onCreate(savedInstanceState);
    setContentView(R.layout.activity_main);

    . . .
}
```

onStart(): This method is called when an activity becomes visible to the user. This method can be used for start-up activities, such as registering services, initializing objects, and so forth. In the example below, an activity `onStart()` method is used to initialize the event bus.

```
public void onStart() {
    EventBus.getDefault().register(this);
    super.onStart();
}
```

onStop(): This method is called when an activity is not visible to the user. This method can be used for cleanup activities such as closing connections, reinitializing objects, and so forth. In the following example, an activity `onStop()` method is used to stop the event bus.

```
public void onStop() {
    EventBus.getDefault().unregister(this);
    super.onStop();
}
```

onRestart(): This method is called when you restart a stopped activity. See the following example.

```
@Override
protected void onRestart() {
    . . .
}
```

onResume(): This method is called when you resume the paused activity. The `onResume()` method is called only for a paused activity. An example code is provided below.

```
@Override
protected void onResume() {
    ...
}
```

onPause(): This method called when the current activity is paused, and some other activity is resumed. The `onResume()` method is used to resume the paused activity. An example code is provided below.

```
@Override
protected void onPause() {
    ...
}
```

onDestroy(): This method is called when an activity is finished or destroyed. An example code is provided below.

```
@Override
protected void onDestroy() {
    ...
}
```

Listing 2-1 provides a sample activity class with life cycle methods.

Listing 2-1: MainActivity.java class.

```
package com.learning.android.androidbasics;

import android.app.Activity;
import android.os.Bundle;

// MyFirstActivity.java
public class MyFirstActivity extends Activity {

    @Override
    protected void onCreate(Bundle savedInstanceState) {
        System.out.println("------ onCreate() is called ------");
    }

    @Override
    protected void onStart() {
        System.out.println("------ onStart() is called ------");
    }

    @Override
    protected void onRestart() {
        System.out.println("------ onRestart() is called ------");
    }

    @Override
    protected void onResume() {
        System.out.println("------ onResume() is called ------");
    }
```

```java
    @Override
    protected void onPause() {
        System.out.println("------ onPause() is called ------");
    }

    @Override
    protected void onStop() {
        System.out.println("------ onStop() is called ------");
    }

    @Override
    protected void onDestroy() {
        System.out.println("------ onDestroy() is called ------");
    }
}
```

Figure 2-1 shows an activity life cycle.

Figure 2-1: Life cycle of an activity from start to destroy

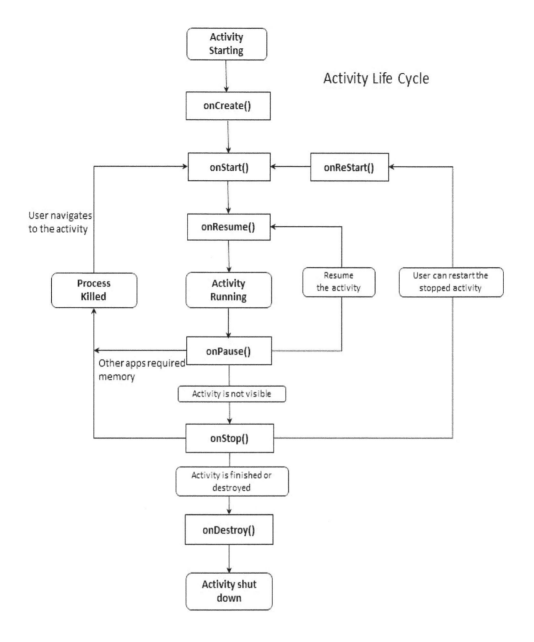

NOTE: Image reproduced from Android open-source project. Refer to API reference documentation for more details. http://developer.android.com/reference/android/app/Activity.html

Activity Components

Some of the most commonly used activity components are listed below.

- List Activity
- ActionBarActivity/AppCompactActivity

List Activity

The `ListActivity` class is used to display collections data. This widget is used for developing list views in Android applications. Your activity class must extend the `ListActivity` class. The `onListItemClick(...)` method is used to handle the list item click event. An example code is provided below.

```
public class ProductActivity extends ListActivity {
    ...

    // Handle the list item click event
    public void onListItemClick(ListView parent, View v,
        int position, long id) {
        ...
    }
}
```

NOTE: Tutorial -4 of Chapter -3 provides the complete details on implementing the list views.

ActionBarActivity/AppCompactActivity

The `ActionBarActivity` and `AppCompactActivity` classes are used to add an action bar to your application. The `ActionBarActivity` class no longer supported in new versions of Android. Newer versions use the `AppCompactActivity` class for adding action bars to your application. You can add menus and icons to the action bar. The rules applying to the menu and menu items are explained below.

- The activity class must extend `AppCompatActivity` class. An example action class code is provided below.
- The action class must override the `onCreateOptionsMenu(...)` and `onOptionsItemSelected(...)` methods. These callback methods handle the menu selection events.

```
public class MainActivity extends AppCompatActivity {

    @Override
    // Inflates the main menu "menu_main.xml" file
    public boolean onCreateOptionsMenu(Menu menu) {
        getMenuInflater().inflate(R.menu.menu_main, menu);

        ...
    }

    @Override
    // Handles menu item click events
    public boolean onOptionsItemSelected(MenuItem item) {
        ...
    }
}
```

NOTE: Tutorial -3 in Chapter -3 provides the complete details on implementing the action bar.

Intents

Intents are used for communicating between two activities. Figure 2-2 shows communication between two activities through an intent. You can pass the data from one activity to another through intents.

Figure 2-2: Activity-to-Activity communication.

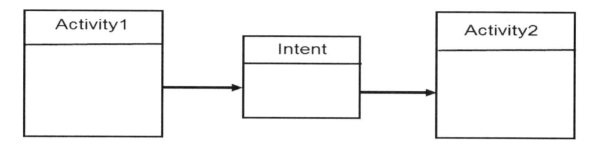

Intent calling Activity2 from Activity1

An example use of an intent is provided below. The `startActivity()` method of an `Activity` class is used to call the other activity class. In the following example, the `MainActivity` class is calling the `ProductActivity` class.

```
public class MainActivity extends Activity {

    . . .

    public void CallProducts(View view) {
        Intent intent = new Intent(this, ProductActivity.class);
        startActivity(intent);
    }
}
```

The `putExtra(...)` method of an intent class is used to pass data from one activity to another. See the below provided example.

```
Intent intent = new Intent(this, ProductDetailsActivity.class);
intent.putExtra("productName", "Vector Calculus");
startActivity(intent);
```

The `getExtra(...)` method of an intent class is used to get data that has been already set. An example code is provided below.

```
String productName = getIntent().getStringExtra("productName");
```

NOTE: Tutorial -5 of Chapter -3 provides the complete details on implementing the activities and intents.

Fragments

Figure 2-3 shows the relationship between an activity and a fragment. Fragments were introduced in Android 3.0 for the purpose of effectively utilizing the screen space of the devices. The characteristics of a fragment are listed below.

- An activity can contain one or many fragments.
- Fragments are like multiple sections inside an activity.
- A fragment can contain one or many views (widgets).
- Each fragment will have its own life cycle.
- A fragment will always be embedded inside an activity.
- The two fragments in an activity can communicate with each other.
- When an activity is destroyed, all its embedded fragments will be destroyed.
- Your fragment class must extend the `android.app.Fragment` class

Figure 2-3: Fragments embedded in an activity

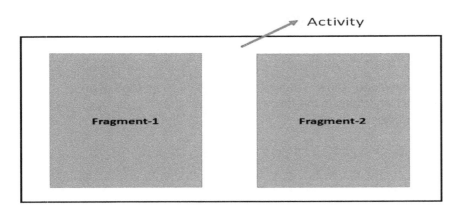

Activity with two Fragments

The layout shown below contains two fragments; one is called `MasterFragment`, and the other is `DetailFragment`. These two fragments are embedded in an activity layout file. The activity class renders this layout file. This layout file is named "fragment_activity.xml".

```xml
<?xml version="1.0" encoding="utf-8"?>
<LinearLayout
    xmlns:android="http://schemas.android.com/apk/res/android"
    android:layout_width="fill_parent"
    android:layout_height="fill_parent"
    android:orientation="vertical" >

    <fragment
        android:id="@+id/master_Fragment"
        android:layout_width="0dp"
        android:layout_height="match_parent"
        android:layout_weight="1"
        android:name="com.example.andriodlearning.MasterFragment"/>

    <fragment
```

```
            android:id="@+id/detail_Fragment"
            android:layout_width="0dp"
            android:layout_height="match_parent"
            android:layout_weight="2"
            android:name="com.example.andriodlearning.DetailFragment"/>

</LinearLayout>
```

An example activity class code is provided below. This activity class renders the previously created layout file "fragment_activity.xml".

```
public class FragmentsActivity extends Activity {

    @Override
    protected void onCreate(Bundle savedInstanceState) {
        super.onCreate(savedInstanceState);
        setContentView(R.layout.fragment_activity);
    }
}
```

An example layout with three buttons is provided below, named "master_fragment.xml". The MasterFragment class inflates the following layout.

```
<?xml version="1.0" encoding="utf-8"?>
<LinearLayout
    xmlns:android="http://schemas.android.com/apk/res/android"
    android:layout_width="match_parent"
    android:layout_height="match_parent"
    android:background="#CCFF99"
    android:orientation="vertical"
    android:padding="5dp">

    <Button
        android:id="@+id/android_btn_id"
        android:layout_width="wrap_content"
        android:layout_height="wrap_content"
        android:text="Android"/>

    <Button
        android:id="@+id/ios_btn_id"
        android:layout_width="wrap_content"
        android:layout_height="wrap_content"
        android:text="IOS"/>

    <Button
        android:id="@+id/windows_btn_id"
        android:layout_width="wrap_content"
        android:layout_height="wrap_content"
        android:text="Windows"/>

</LinearLayout>
```

An example MasterFragment class code is provided below. This fragment class inflates the previously created "master_fragment.xml" file.

```
public class MasterFragment extends Fragment implements
```

```
                    View.OnClickListener {

        @Override
        public View onCreateView(LayoutInflater inflater,
                            ViewGroup container,
                            Bundle savedInstanceState) {
            View view = inflater.inflate(R.layout.master_fragment,
                            container, false);

            ...

        }
}
```

An example layout with one text field is provided below. This layout is named "detail_fargment.xml".
The `DetailFragment` class inflates this layout file.

```
<?xml version="1.0" encoding="utf-8"?>
<LinearLayout
    xmlns:android="http://schemas.android.com/apk/res/android"
    android:layout_width="match_parent"
    android:layout_height="match_parent"
    android:background="#FFFF99"
    android:orientation="vertical"
    android:padding="20dp" >

    <TextView
        android:id="@+id/display_tv"
        android:layout_width="wrap_content"
        android:layout_height="wrap_content"
        android:text=""
        android:textSize="40sp" />

</LinearLayout>
```

An example `DetailFragment` class code is provided below. This fragment class inflates the
previously created "detail_fragment.xml" file.

```
public class DetailFragment extends Fragment {

    @Override
    public View onCreateView(LayoutInflater inflater,
                        ViewGroup container,
                        Bundle savedInstanceState) {
        View view = inflater.inflate(R.layout.detail_fragment,
                            container, false);

        ...

        return view;
    }
}
```

NOTE: Tutorial 3 in Chapter 5 provides the complete details on implementing the fragments.

Fragment Life Cycle

Like the activity class, the fragment class will have its own life cycle. Fragments are embedded inside activities, and the class has the following life cycle methods.

- onCreate()
- onCreateView()
- onAttach()
- onActivityCreated()
- onStart()
- onResume()
- onPause()
- onStop()
- onDestroyView()
- onDestroy()
- onDetach()

Listing 2-2 shows an example fragment class with life cycle methods.

Listing 2-2: MyFirstFragment.java class.

```
package com.learning.android.androidbasics;

import android.app.Fragment;
import android.os.Bundle;
import android.view.LayoutInflater;
import android.view.View;
import android.view.ViewGroup;

// MyFirstFragment.java
public class MyFirstFragment extends Fragment {

    @Override
    public View onCreateView(LayoutInflater inflater,
                        ViewGroup container,
                        Bundle savedInstanceState) {

        ...

        return null;
    }

    @Override
    public void onCreate(android.os.Bundle savedInstanceState) {
        super.onCreate(savedInstanceState);
    }

    @Override
    public void onAttach(android.content.Context context) {
        super.onAttach(context);
    }

    @Override
    public void onActivityCreated(Bundle savedInstanceState) {
        super.onActivityCreated(savedInstanceState);
    }
```

```
    @Override
    public void onStart() {
        super.onStart();
    }

    @Override
    public void onResume() {
        super.onResume();
    }

    @Override
    public void onPause() {
        super.onPause();
    }

    @Override
    public void onStop() {
        super.onStop();
    }

    @Override
    public void onDestroyView() {
        super.onDestroyView();
    }

    @Override
    public void onDestroy() {
        super.onDestroy();
    }

    @Override
    public void onDetach() {
        super.onDetach();
    }
}
```

The life cycle of a fragment will have an effect on the state of an activity. The following table shows each fragment life cycle method and its effect on activity life cycle.

Activity State	Fragment life cycle methods
Created	onCreate() onCreateView() onAttach() onActivityCreated()
Started	onStart()
Resumed	onResume()
Paused	onPause()
Stopped	onStop()
Destroyed	onDestroyView() onDestroy() onDetach()

Summary

Figure 2-4 summarizes the most important points described in this chapter.

- Activities are used for building the user interface. Activity classes render the XML layout file.
- Intents are used for communicating between two activities. You can pass the data from one activity to another using an intent.
- Fragments act like multiple sections inside an activity. Fragments are embedded inside an activity.

Figure 2-4 Activities, Intents, and Fragments

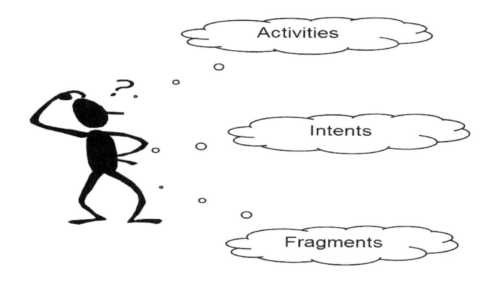

Chapter 3. My First Android Project

Android provides several widgets and user interface controls, such as text control, edit text, radio group, checkboxes, spinner, progress dialog, and so forth. This chapter will help you to understand the commonly used user interface controls and widgets in Android development.

This chapter will discuss the following topics:

- How to use views and view groups
- The commonly used user interface widgets in Android.
- Understanding the Android project structure, files, and folders. Develop your first Android project.
- Developing menus, menu items, list view, and action bar widgets.
- How to use various types of activities and intents
- How to pass data from one activity to another.

Commonly Used UI Widgets (Views)

The section illustrates the user interface (UI) controls most commonly used in Android application development. The complete list of Android widgets would be very big, but this section covers only a few of them. Figure 3.1 shows the commonly used user interface widgets.

Figure 3-1: Android UI widgets

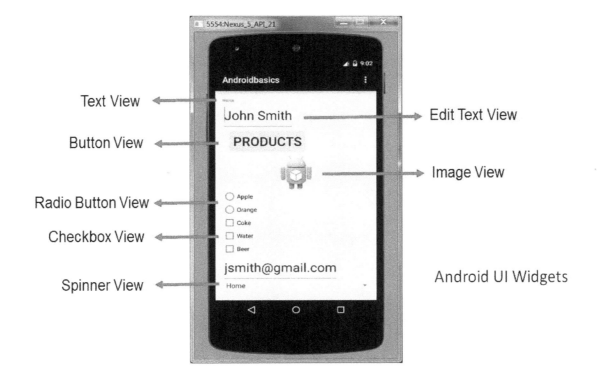

The following section illustrates the use of each widget in greater detail.

Text View

Text view defines the label for an input text field. The attributes of the text view are self-explanatory. An example code of a text view is given below.

```
<TextView
    android:id="@+id/name"
    android:layout_width="fill_parent"
    android:layout_height="fill_parent"
    android:text="Name"
    android:textSize="30px"
    android:textStyle="bold"/>
```

Edit Text

Edit text view allows the user to enter data either on a single line or on multiple lines. An example of edit text view is provided below.

```
<EditText
    android:id="@+id/username_edittext"
    android:layout_width="wrap_content"
    android:layout_height="wrap_content"
    android:layout_marginTop="5dp"
    android:text="John Smith"
    android:enabled="true"
    android:textSize="30sp"/>
```

Image View

Image view allows the user to view images. The following code loads the image "ic_launcher.png" from the "drawable" directory.

```
<ImageView
    android:id="@+id/greenrobot"
    android:layout_width="250px"
    android:layout_height="250px"
    android:layout_gravity="center"
    android:scaleType="fitCenter"
    android:src="@drawable/ic_launcher"/>
```

Button

Button view is used for user actions. A button consists of a text box or icon. Buttons respond to user click events. Below provided code example, the button executes the "onCLick" event; and invokes the "CallProducts" method of an action class.

```
<Button
```

```
        android:id="@+id/products_button"
        android:layout_width="wrap_content"
        android:layout_height="wrap_content"
        android:layout_marginBottom="5sp"
        android:layout_marginLeft="12dp"
        android:layout_marginRight="12dp"
        android:enabled="true"
        android:text="Products"
        android:textSize="30sp"
        android:onClick="CallProducts"/>
```

The corresponding method in the action class is provided below.

```
public void CallProducts(View view) {
    Intent intent = new Intent(this, ProductActivity.class);
    startActivity(intent);
}
```

Alternatively, the user can add a Listener to the button-click event. An example code is provided below.

```
Button productsButton = (Button) findViewById(R.id.products_button);
productsButton.setEnabled(true);
productsButton.setOnClickListener(productsButtonListener);
```

The following method receives the button-click event. An example code is provided below.

```
private View.OnClickListener productsButtonListener = new
    View.OnClickListener() {
    public void onClick(View v) {
        ...
    }
}
```

Menus, Menu Items, and the Action Bar.

Menus are a commonly used component of user interfaces, which allow users to choose one option form a given list of options. A menu contains a list of menu items. Menus are attached to an action bar. The following approaches can be used to create menus in Android:

1. XML-based configuration.
2. Add menu and menu items programmatically.

In case of XML-based configurations, you can add menu items to the "menu_main.xml" file. This file is available inside the "menu" directory. Inflate this XML file inside your action class.

```
<?xml version="1.0" encoding="utf-8"?>
<menu xmlns:android="http://schemas.android.com/apk/res/android"
    xmlns:app="http://schemas.android.com/apk/res-auto"
    android:layout_width="match_parent"
    android:layout_height="wrap_content">

    <item
```

```
        android:id="@+id/new_game"
        android:icon="@drawable/apple"
        android:title="Item 1"
        app:showAsAction="ifRoom"/>

    <item
        android:id="@+id/help"
        android:icon="@drawable/cherry"
        android:title="Item 2"
        app:showAsAction="always"/>
</menu>
```

Use the following approach to add a menu and menu items programmatically to an action bar.

- The activity class must extend `AppCompatActivity` class. Older versions of the Android API provide `ActionBarActivity`, but this class is deprecated.
- The action class must override the `onCreateOptionsMenu(...)` and `onOptionsItemSelected(...)` methods. These callback methods receive the menu selection events.

The following action class extends the `AppCompatActivity`.

```
public class MainActivity extends AppCompatActivity {
    ...
}
```

The below provided method inflates the menu and adds items to the action bar, if it is present.

```
@Override
public boolean onCreateOptionsMenu(Menu menu) {

    getMenuInflater().inflate(R.menu.menu_main, menu);

    menu.add(0, 0, 0, "Item 1");
    menu.add(0, 1, 1, "Item 2");
    menu.add(0, 2, 2, "Item 3");
    menu.add(0, 3, 3, "Item 4");
    menu.add(0, 4, 4, "Item 5");
    menu.add(0, 5, 5, "Item 6");
    menu.add(0, 6, 6, "Item 7");
}
```

The below provided method handles click events in action bar items.

```
@Override
public boolean onOptionsItemSelected(MenuItem item) {

    switch (item.getItemId()) {
        case 0:
            Toast.makeText(this, "You clicked on Item 1",
                    Toast.LENGTH_LONG).show();
            return true;
        case 1:
            Toast.makeText(this, "You clicked on Item 2",
                    Toast.LENGTH_LONG).show();
```

```
                return true;
        case 2:
                Toast.makeText(this, "You clicked on Item 3",
                        Toast.LENGTH_LONG).show();
                return true;
    }

    return false;
}
```

Radio Group and Radio Buttons

Radio group view allow the user to select one option from a given set. This view shows all the available options to the user, and the users select only one. Radio group view supports both vertical and horizontal orientations.

The following code shows an example of radio group view.

```
<RadioGroup
    android:layout_width="fill_parent"
    android:layout_height="wrap_content"
    android:orientation="vertical">

        <RadioButton android:id="@+id/radio_applepirates"
            android:layout_width="wrap_content"
            android:layout_height="wrap_content"
            android:text="Apple"
            android:onClick="onRadioButtonClicked"/>

        <RadioButton android:id="@+id/radio_orange"
            android:layout_width="wrap_content"
            android:layout_height="wrap_content"
            android:text="Orange"
            android:onClick="onRadioButtonClicked"/>

</RadioGroup>
```

The following method handles the radio button click event.

```
public void onRadioButtonClicked(View view) {
    switch(view.getId()) {
        ...
    }
}
```

Checkbox

Checkbox view allow the user to select one or more options from a given set. The checkbox view shows all available options to the user; users can choose one or many of them. This view supports both vertical and horizontal orientations.

An example of check box view is provided below.

```
<CheckBox android:id="@+id/checkbox_coke"
    android:layout_width="wrap_content"
    android:layout_height="wrap_content"
    android:text="Coke"
    android:onClick="onCheckboxClicked"/>

<CheckBox android:id="@+id/checkbox_water"
    android:layout_width="wrap_content"
    android:layout_height="wrap_content"
    android:text="Water"
    android:onClick="onCheckboxClicked"/>

<CheckBox android:id="@+id/checkbox_beer"
    android:layout_width="wrap_content"
    android:layout_height="wrap_content"
    android:text="Beer"
    android:onClick="onCheckboxClicked"/>
```

The following method handles a checkbox click event.

```
public void onCheckboxClicked(View view) {
    switch(view.getId()) {
        . . .
    }
}
```

Spinner

Spinner view works the same way as an HTML list box element. It shows the list of items, and the user can choose one of them. Figure 3-2 shows an example Spinner view.

Figure 3-2: Spinner widget

The following layout is used to create a Spinner view.

```
<LinearLayout
    android:layout_width="match_parent"
    android:layout_height="wrap_content"
```

Commonly Used UI Widgets (Views)

```
    android:layout_gravity="center_horizontal"
    android:orientation="vertical">

<EditText
    android:id="@+id/mail_edittext"
    android:layout_width="wrap_content"
    android:layout_height="wrap_content"
    android:layout_marginTop="5dp"
    android:text="jsmith@gmail.com"
    android:enabled="true"
    android:textSize="30sp" />

<Spinner
    android:id="@+id/email_spinner"
    android:layout_width="fill_parent"
    android:layout_height="wrap_content" />

</LinearLayout>
```

Add the following data to your "strings.xml" file.

```
<string-array name="email_array">
    <item>Home</item>
    <item>Office</item>
    <item>Personnel</item>
    <item>Dummy</item>
</string-array>
```

Adding the following code in your activity class, this code adds a spinner to your screen.

```
// Create a spinner view
Spinner spinner = (Spinner) findViewById(R.id.email_spinner);

/* Create an ArrayAdapter using the string array
    and a default spinner layout */
ArrayAdapter<CharSequence> adapter =
    ArrayAdapter.createFromResource(this,
    R.array.email_array,
    android.R.layout.simple_spinner_item);

// Specify the layout to use when the list of choices appears
adapter.setDropDownViewResource(
    android.R.layout.simple_spinner_dropdown_item);

// Apply the adapter to the spinner
spinner.setAdapter(adapter);
```

Progress Dialog

Android's ProgressDialog class is used to show the progress dialogs for long running operations. The following code is used to show the progress bar.

```
progressBar.show();
```

The following code hides the progress bar.

```
progressBar.hide();
```

The following code kills the progress bar.

```
progressBar.dismiss();
```

An example of how to use progress bar in an application is provided below.

```
ProgressDialog progressBar = new ProgressDialog(v.getContext());
progressBar.setCancelable(true);
progressBar.setMessage("Processing ...");
progressBar.setProgressStyle(ProgressDialog.STYLE_SPINNER);
progressBar.setProgress(0);
progressBar.setMax(100);
progressBar.show();
```

Layout Managers/View Groups

A view group can contain collection of views (UI elements). The commonly used view groups in Android are listed below.

- Linear layout
- Relative layout
- Grid layout
- Table layout
- Drawer layout
- Frame layout

Linear Layout

Linear layout arranges the user interface controls (views) in single row or column. It supports both vertical and horizontal orientations. All views in the linear layout follow one after another, either vertically or horizontally.

In a vertical orientation, the layout will have only one view per row. Here's an example of the XML for a linear layout.

```
<LinearLayout xmlns:android="http://schemas.android.com/apk/res/android"
    xmlns:tools="http://schemas.android.com/tools"
    android:layout_width="match_parent"
    android:layout_height="wrap_content"
    android:orientation="vertical">

    ...

    /* Include UI controls such as buttons, text fields, widgets,
       and so forth */

</LinearLayout>
```

The linear layout provided below arranges the user interface controls in a vertical direction.

```xml
<LinearLayout xmlns:android="http://schemas.android.com/apk/res/android"
    xmlns:tools="http://schemas.android.com/tools"
    android:layout_width="match_parent"
    android:layout_height="wrap_content"
    android:orientation="vertical">

        <TextView
            android:id="@+id/show_message"
            android:layout_width="wrap_content"
            android:layout_height="wrap_content"
            android:layout_marginTop="5dp"
            android:enabled="true"
            android:textColor="#ff000000"
            android:text="" />

        <TextView
            android:layout_width="wrap_content"
            android:layout_height="wrap_content"
            android:layout_marginTop="5dp"
            android:enabled="true"
            android:textColor="#ff000000"
            android:text="Username" />

        <EditText
            android:id="@+id/username_edittext"
            android:layout_width="wrap_content"
            android:layout_height="wrap_content"
            android:layout_marginTop="5dp"
            android:enabled="true"
            android:textSize="30sp" />

        <TextView
            android:layout_width="wrap_content"
            android:layout_height="wrap_content"
            android:layout_marginTop="5dp"
            android:enabled="true"
            android:textColor="#ff000000"
            android:text="Password" />

        <EditText
            android:id="@+id/password_editpass"
            android:layout_width="wrap_content"
            android:layout_height="wrap_content"
            android:layout_marginTop="5dp"
            android:enabled="true"
            android:textSize="30sp" />

        <Button
            android:id="@+id/login_button"
            android:layout_width="wrap_content"
            android:layout_height="wrap_content"
            android:text="Login"
            android:textSize="30sp" />

</LinearLayout>
```

Figure 3-3 shows the output of the code shown above.

Figure 3-3: Linear layout in a vertical orientation

Similarly, the linear layout shown below arranges the user interface controls in a horizontal direction.

```
<LinearLayout xmlns:android="http://schemas.android.com/apk/res/android"
    xmlns:tools="http://schemas.android.com/tools"
    android:layout_width="match_parent"
    android:layout_height="wrap_content"
    android:orientation="horizontal">

    // Add your UI elements here

</LinearLayout>
```

Figure 3-4 shows the output of the code shown above.

Figure 3-4: Linear layout in a horizontal orientation

Relative Layout

Relative layout is a view group which arranges views in relative positions. Android provides attributes such as left, right, center, above, and so forth. These attributes are used to arrange the views as relative to other views. These attributes are listed below.

```
android:layout_below
android:layout_above
android:layout_centerHorizontal
android:layout_alignParentLeft
android:layout_toLeftOf
android:layout_alignParentRight
```

In the following example, "username" text view is arranged below the "show_message" view, and to the left of the "user name" edit text.

```
<TextView
     android:layout_width="wrap_content"
     android:layout_height="wrap_content"
     android:layout_marginTop="5dp"
     android:enabled="true"
     android:textColor="#ff000000"
     android:layout_below="@id/show_message"
     android:layout_alignParentLeft="true"
     android:layout_toLeftOf="@+id/username_edittext"
     android:text="Username" />
```

The below provided relative layout arranges the views in relative positions. The complete XML file is shown below.

```xml
<RelativeLayout xmlns:android =
    "http://schemas.android.com/apk/res/android"
    xmlns:tools="http://schemas.android.com/tools"
    android:layout_width="match_parent"
    android:layout_height="wrap_content"
    tools:context=".MainActivity">

    <TextView
        android:id="@+id/show_message"
        android:layout_width="wrap_content"
        android:layout_height="wrap_content"
        android:layout_marginTop="5dp"
        android:textColor="#ff000000"
        android:text="Message" />

    <TextView
        android:layout_width="wrap_content"
        android:layout_height="wrap_content"
        android:textColor="#ff000000"
        android:layout_below="@id/show_message"
        android:layout_alignParentLeft="true"
        android:layout_toLeftOf="@+id/username_edittext"
        android:text="@string/username" />

    <EditText
        android:id="@+id/username_edittext"
        android:layout_width="wrap_content"
        android:layout_height="wrap_content"
        android:enabled="true"
        android:layout_below="@id/show_message"
        android:layout_alignParentRight="true"
        android:textSize="30sp" />

    <Button
        android:id="@+id/login_button"
        android:layout_width="wrap_content"
        android:layout_height="wrap_content"
        android:enabled="true"
        android:layout_below="@id/username_edittext"
        android:layout_alignParentRight="true"
        android:text="@string/login"/>

</RelativeLayout>
```

Figure 3-5 shows the resulting views with relative layout view group.

Figure 3-5: Relative layout

Grid Layout

Grid layout is a view group which arranges views in rows and columns. This layout arranges the views into a two-dimensional matrix structure. An example of the grid view layout is provided below.

```xml
<?xml version="1.0" encoding="utf-8"?>
<GridView xmlns:android="http://schemas.android.com/apk/res/android"
    android:id="@+id/gridview"
    android:layout_width="match_parent"
    android:layout_height="match_parent"
    android:columnWidth="90dp"
    android:numColumns="auto_fit"
    android:verticalSpacing="10dp"
    android:horizontalSpacing="10dp"
    android:stretchMode="columnWidth"
    android:gravity="center"/>
```

The following code renders the above grid layout.

```java
@Override
protected void onCreate(Bundle savedInstanceState) {
    super.onCreate(savedInstanceState);
    setContentView(R.layout.activity_main);

    String[] numbers = new String[] {
        "1", "2", "3", "4",
        "5", "6", "7", "8",
        "9", "10", "11", "12"
    };
```

```
GridView gridView = (GridView) findViewById(R.id.gridview);
ArrayAdapter<String> adapter = new ArrayAdapter<String>(this,
            android.R.layout.simple_list_item_1, numbers);

gridView.setAdapter(adapter);
}
```

Figure 3-6 shows the output view of a grid layout.

Figure 3-6: Grid layout

Table Layout

The structure of the table layout is same as HTML table. A table which contains both rows and columns. Each row can have one or more columns. A <TableRow> element is used to create a row inside the table layout. An example use of table view layout is shown below.

```
<?xml version="1.0" encoding="utf-8"?>
<TableLayout xmlns:android="http://schemas.android.com/apk/res/android"
    android:layout_width="match_parent"
    android:layout_height="match_parent"
    android:stretchColumns="1">

    <!-- two columns -->
    <TableRow>
        <TextView
            android:text="Samsung"
            android:textColor="#ff000000"
            android:padding="3dip" />
```

```
        <TextView
            android:text="Android"
            android:gravity="right"
            android:textColor="#ff000000"
            android:padding="3dip" />
    </TableRow>

    <!-- two columns -->
    <TableRow>
        <TextView
            android:text="iPhone"
            android:textColor="#ff000000"
            android:padding="3dip" />
        <TextView
            android:text="iOS"
            android:textColor="#ff000000"
            android:gravity="right"
            android:padding="3dip" />
    </TableRow>

    <!-- draw a red line -->
    <View
        android:layout_height="2dip"
        android:background="#FF0000" />

    <!-- 1 column and 1 row -->
    <TableRow>
        <TextView
            android:text="Nexus"
            android:textColor="#ff000000"
            android:padding="3dip" />
    </TableRow>

    <!-- draw a red line -->
    <View
        android:layout_height="2dip"
        android:textColor="#ff000000"
        android:background="#FF0000" />

</TableLayout>
```

Figure 3-7 shows the output view of a table layout.

Figure 3-7: Table layout

Frame Layout

Frame Layout is a view group which is used to block out an area to display a single view. It acts as a container for single view. An example use of frame view layout is shown below.

```
<FrameLayout xmlns:android="http://schemas.android.com/apk/res/android"
    android:layout_width="fill_parent"
    android:layout_height="fill_parent"
    android:id="@+id/framelayout">

    <ImageView
        android:id="@+id/greenrobo"
        android:src="@drawable/ic_launcher"
        android:scaleType="fitCenter"
        android:layout_height="250px"
        android:layout_width="250px"
        android:layout_gravity="center"/>

</FrameLayout>
```

Figure 3-8 shows the output view of a frame layout.

Figure 3-8: Frame layout

Drawer Layout

Figure 3-9 shows the navigation drawer layout.

Figure 3-9: Drawer layout

The navigation drawer layout is most commonly found pattern in Google applications which slides from left to right with a toggled hamburger icon on the toolbar. A drawer layout is used for navigating to various pages in your application.

An example of a drawer layout widget is shown below.

```
<android.support.v4.widget.DrawerLayout
    xmlns:android="http://schemas.android.com/apk/res/android"
    xmlns:app="http://schemas.android.com/apk/res-auto"
    xmlns:tools="http://schemas.android.com/tools"
    android:id="@+id/drawer_layout"
    android:layout_width="match_parent"
    android:layout_height="match_parent">
```

NOTE: Chapter -10 provides the complete implementation details for navigation drawer.

My First Android Project

Tutorial 1: Creating your First Android Project

To create your first Android project, follow the step-by-step instructions provided below.

Step 1: Open your Android studio. Go to File → New Project. Refer to Figure 3-10

Figure 3-10: Creating a new Android project

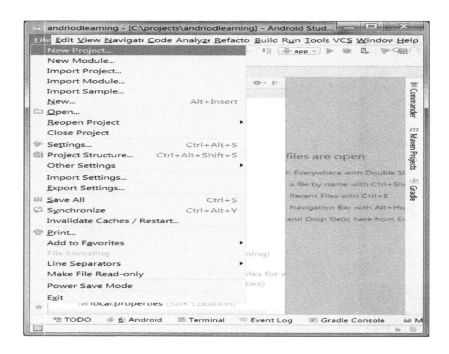

Step 2: The New Project window will be shown. Enter the details as shown in Figure 3-11, then click Next.

Figure 3-11: Configure project details

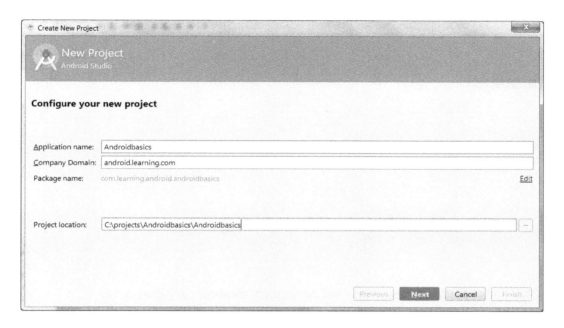

Step 3: The Activity window will appear. Select the blank activity, as shown in shown in Figure 3-12, then click Next.

Figure 3-12: Choose activity template class

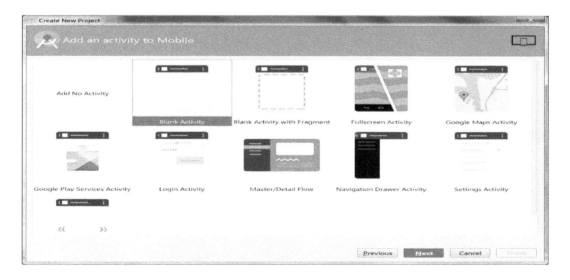

Step 4: The activity metadata window will be open. Leave the default names as shown in Figure 3-13

Figure 3-13: Activity details

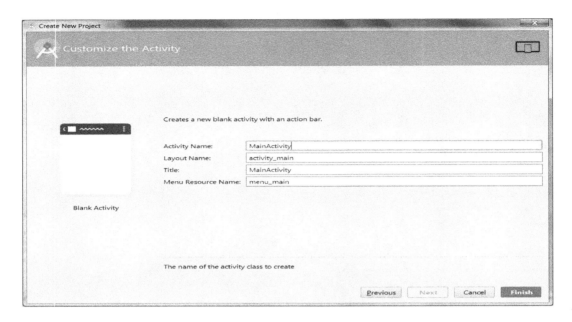

Step 5: Click Finish button. A new project will be created, as shown in Figure 3-14.

Figure 3-14: Project explorer in Android studio

Step 6: Run the project.

View the output on the console. If you see the following error while running the project, update the emulator command line options.

Emulator: emulator window was out of view and was recentered

FATAL:.//android/base/sockets/SocketWaiter.cpp:88:Check failed: isValidFd(fd). fd 1060 max1024

Go to Edit Configurations and update the emulator command line options as shown in Figure 3-15.

Open Edit Configurations window. Run → Edit Configurations. Add the following additional command line parameters as shown in Figure 3-15.

-no-audio –scale 0.30

-no-audio → disables the audio on you emulator device

-scale 0.30 → reduces the size of the emulator device. Use this based on your screen size.

Figure 3-15: Window shows emulator command line options

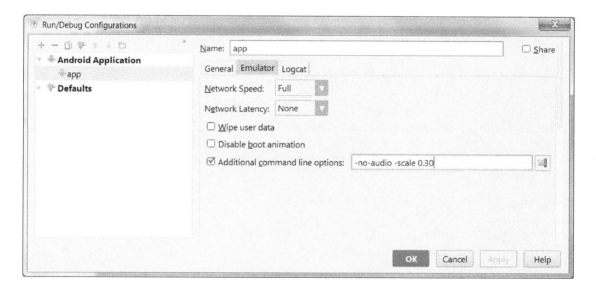

Step 7: View the output in emulator.

Run the project. You can view the output on emulator screen, as shown in Figure 3-16.

Figure 3-16: Output shown on emulator screen

Tutorials

Tutorial 2: Customizing your First Android Project – Login/Password

In this tutorial, you will add more user interface controls to your application. Implement the following business scenario.

Use Case Scenario:

- Add "User Name" label and edit text control
- Add "Password" label and edit text control
- Add "LogIn" button on your screen.
- Enter valid user name and password → Click on "LogIn" button.
- Display success/failure message to the user.

The navigation scenario described above is shown in Figure 3-17.

Figure 3-17: LogIn/Password screen

The steps required to implement the business scenario outlined above in Android are listed below:

1. Add the required labels.
2. Update the main activity layout file.
3. Run the application.
4. Update the main activity class.
5. Run the application.

These steps are described in the following sections:

Step 1: Add required labels

Add the required labels to the "strings.xml" file. Go to res → val → strings.xml file. Open "strings.xml" file. Add the following labels.

```
<string name="username">User Name</string>
<string name="password">Password</string>
<string name="login">Login</string>
```

Step 2: Update a main activity layout file

Here, reuse the "activity_main.xml" file that we created in Tutorial -1. Open the main activity layout file. Go to res → layout directory, update the "activity_main.xml" file.

Add the following user interface elements to the main activity layout file. The following element adds a "User Name" label. Add the required labels to the "strings.xml" file.

```
<TextView
     android:layout_width="match_parent"
     android:layout_height="wrap_content"
```

```
        android:layout_marginTop="5dp"
        android:enabled="true"
        android:textColor="#ff000000"
        android:text="@string/username" />
```

The following element adds a user name edit text element.

```
<EditText
        android:id="@+id/username_edittext"
        android:layout_width="match_parent"
        android:layout_height="wrap_content"
        android:layout_marginTop="5dp"
        android:enabled="true"
        android:textSize="30sp"/>
```

Follow the same process to, add the password label and edit text elements to your main activity layout file.

The following element adds a "LogIn" button element.

```
<Button
        android:id="@+id/login_button"
        android:layout_width="match_parent"
        android:layout_height="wrap_content"
        android:layout_marginBottom="5sp"
        android:layout_marginLeft="12dp"
        android:layout_marginRight="12dp"
        android:enabled="true"
        android:text="@string/login"
        android:textSize="30sp" />
```

The complete "activity_main.xml" file is provided below.

```
<RelativeLayout xmlns:android=
        "http://schemas.android.com/apk/res/android"
        xmlns:tools="http://schemas.android.com/tools"
        android:layout_width="match_parent"
        android:layout_height="match_parent"
        android:paddingBottom="@dimen/activity_vertical_margin"
        android:paddingLeft="@dimen/activity_horizontal_margin"
        android:paddingRight="@dimen/activity_horizontal_margin"
        android:paddingTop="@dimen/activity_vertical_margin"
        tools:context=".MainActivity">

    <LinearLayout
        android:layout_width="match_parent"
        android:layout_height="wrap_content"
        android:layout_gravity="center_horizontal"
        android:orientation="vertical">

        <TextView
            android:id="@+id/show_message"
            android:layout_width="match_parent"
            android:layout_height="wrap_content"
            android:layout_marginTop="5dp"
            android:enabled="true"
```

```
            android:textColor="#ff000000"
            android:text="" />

        <TextView
            android:layout_width="match_parent"
            android:layout_height="wrap_content"
            android:layout_marginTop="5dp"
            android:enabled="true"
            android:textColor="#ff000000"
            android:text="@string/username" />

        <EditText
            android:id="@+id/username_edittext"
            android:layout_width="match_parent"
            android:layout_height="wrap_content"
            android:layout_marginTop="5dp"
            android:enabled="true"
            android:textSize="30sp" />

        <TextView
            android:layout_width="match_parent"
            android:layout_height="wrap_content"
            android:layout_marginTop="5dp"
            android:enabled="true"
            android:textColor="#ff000000"
            android:text="@string/password" />

        <EditText
            android:id="@+id/password_editpass"
            android:layout_width="match_parent"
            android:layout_height="wrap_content"
            android:layout_marginTop="5dp"
            android:enabled="true"
            android:textSize="30sp" />

        <Button
            android:id="@+id/login_button"
            android:layout_width="match_parent"
            android:layout_height="wrap_content"
            android:layout_marginBottom="5sp"
            android:layout_marginLeft="12dp"
            android:layout_marginRight="12dp"
            android:enabled="true"
            android:text="@string/login"
            android:textSize="30sp" />
    </LinearLayout>

</RelativeLayout>
```

Step 3: Run the application.

Run the application and view the user interface in the emulator. Figure 3-18 shows the output.

Figure 3-18: LogIn/Password screen

Step 4: Update the main activity class

Update the main activity class. Implement your business logic in `MainActivity.java`. This activity class renders the "activity_main.xml" layout file.

The following code adds a button-click listener to the "LogIn" button.

```
Button logInButton = (Button) findViewById(R.id.login_button);
logInButton.setEnabled(true);
logInButton.setOnClickListener(logInButtonListener);
```

The following method receives the button-click event. Implement your business logic inside this method.

```
private View.OnClickListener logInButtonListener = new
                View.OnClickListener() {
    public void onClick(View v) {
        ...
    }
}
```

Listing 3.1 provides the complete main activity class code.

Listing 3-1: MainActivity.java class.

```
package com.learning.android.androidbasics;

import android.os.Bundle;
```

```java
import android.support.v7.app.AppCompatActivity;
import android.view.Menu;
import android.view.MenuItem;
import android.view.View;
import android.widget.Button;
import android.widget.EditText;
import android.widget.TextView;

// MainActivity.java
public class MainActivity extends AppCompatActivity {

    @Override
    protected void onCreate(Bundle savedInstanceState) {
        super.onCreate(savedInstanceState);
        setContentView(R.layout.activity_main);

        Button logInButton = (Button) findViewById(R.id.login_button);
        logInButton.setEnabled(true);
        logInButton.setOnClickListener(logInButtonListener);
    }

    // Create an anonymous class to act as a button click listener
    private View.OnClickListener logInButtonListener = new
        View.OnClickListener() {
        public void onClick(View v) {
            EditText username = (EditText)
                    findViewById(R.id.username_edittext);
            String userNameTxt = username.getText().toString().trim();

            EditText password = (EditText)
                    findViewById(R.id.password_editpass);
            String passwordTxt = password.getText().toString();

            String message = "";
            if( ("john".equalsIgnoreCase(userNameTxt)) &&
                ("admin123".equalsIgnoreCase(passwordTxt)) ) {
                message = "Valid";
            } else {
                message = "Invalid";
            }

            TextView messageView = (TextView)
                    findViewById(R.id.show_message);
            messageView.setText(message);
        }
    };

    @Override
    public boolean onCreateOptionsMenu(Menu menu) {
        getMenuInflater().inflate(R.menu.menu_main, menu);
        return true;
    }

    @Override
    public boolean onOptionsItemSelected(MenuItem item) {
        int id = item.getItemId();
        if (id == R.id.action_settings) {
```

```
            return true;
        }
        return super.onOptionsItemSelected(item);
    }
}
```

Step 5: Run the application.

Run the application to view the screen in emulator. Follow the step-by-step instructions provided below.

1. Enter user name = "john" and password = "admin123" → Click on "LogIn" → Displays a "Valid" message on the screen (refer to Figure 3-19)
2. Enter user name = "john" and password = "admin12" → Click on "LogIn" → Displays a "Invalid" message on the screen (refer to Figure 3-19)

Figure 3-19: Login/password validation message

Menus

Tutorial 3: Creating Menus and Menu Items

In this tutorial, add a menu and menu items to your application. Implement the following business scenario.

Use Case Scenario:

*   Add "Menu" to the action bar

- Add "Menu Items" to the action bar
- Handle menu click events and print a message on the screen.

The scenario described above is shown in Figure 3-20.

Figure 3-20: Working with menus and menu items

The steps required to implement the above-specified scenario in Android are listed below:

1. Update main activity class.
2. Run the application.

In this tutorial, reuse the code created in Tutorial -2. Extend the Tutorial -2 and add menu and menu items functionalities to it.

The steps outlined above are described in the following sections:

Step 1: Update main activity class.

Menus are attached to an application bar. The rules apply to the menu and menu items are illustrated below.

- The activity class must extend the `AppCompatActivity` class. An example of an action class code is provided below.
- The action class must override the `onCreateOptionsMenu(...)` and `onOptionsItemSelected(...)` methods. These callback methods receive the menu selection events.

An example use of these methods are provided below.

The below provided method inflates the menu and adds items to the action bar, if one is present.

```
@Override
public boolean onCreateOptionsMenu(Menu menu) {

    getMenuInflater().inflate(R.menu.menu_main, menu);
        ...
}
```

The below provided method handles the action bar item click events.

```
@Override
public boolean onOptionsItemSelected(MenuItem item) {
    ...
}
```

Update the `MainActivity.java` created in Tutorial -2. Listing 3-2 provides the complete main activity class code.

Listing 3-2: MainActivity.java class.

```
package com.learning.android.androidbasics;

import android.os.Bundle;
import android.support.v7.app.AppCompatActivity;
import android.view.Menu;
import android.view.MenuItem;
import android.view.View;
import android.widget.Button;
import android.widget.EditText;
import android.widget.TextView;

// MainActivity.java
public class MainActivity extends AppCompatActivity {

    @Override
    protected void onCreate(Bundle savedInstanceState) {
        super.onCreate(savedInstanceState);
        setContentView(R.layout.activity_main);

        Button logInButton = (Button) findViewById(R.id.login_button);
        logInButton.setEnabled(true);
        logInButton.setOnClickListener(logInButtonListener);
    }

    // create an anonymous class to act as a button click listener
    private View.OnClickListener logInButtonListener = new
        View.OnClickListener() {
        public void onClick(View v) {
            EditText username = (EditText)
                    findViewById(R.id.username_edittext);
            String userNameTxt = username.getText().toString().trim();

            EditText password = (EditText)
                    findViewById(R.id.password_editpass);
            String passwordTxt = password.getText().toString();
```

```java
            String message = "";
            if( ("john".equalsIgnoreCase(userNameTxt)) &&
                ("admin123".equalsIgnoreCase(passwordTxt)) ) {
                message = "Valid";
            } else {
                message = "Invalid";
            }

            TextView messageView = (TextView)
                        findViewById(R.id.show_message);
            messageView.setText(message);
        }
    };

    @Override
    // Inflates the main menu "menu_main.xml" file
    public boolean onCreateOptionsMenu(Menu menu) {
        getMenuInflater().inflate(R.menu.menu_main, menu);
        CreateMenu(menu);
        return true;
    }

    // Adding menu items to a menu programatically
    private void CreateMenu(Menu menu_new) {
        menu_new.add(0, 0, 0, "Item 1");
        menu_new.add(0, 1, 1, "Item 2");
        menu_new.add(0, 2, 2, "Item 3");
        menu_new.add(0, 3, 3, "Item 4");
        menu_new.add(0, 4, 4, "Item 5");
        menu_new.add(0, 5, 5, "Item 6");
        menu_new.add(0, 6, 6, "Item 7");
    }

    @Override
    // Handles menu item click events
    public boolean onOptionsItemSelected(MenuItem item) {
        return menuChoice(item);
    }

    // Implement menu item click functionality here
    private boolean menuChoice(MenuItem item) {
        switch (item.getItemId()) {
            case 0:
                Toast.makeText(this, "You clicked on Item 1",
                        Toast.LENGTH_LONG).show();
                return true;
            case 1:
                Toast.makeText(this, "You clicked on Item 2",
                        Toast.LENGTH_LONG).show();
                return true;
            case 2:
                Toast.makeText(this, "You clicked on Item 3",
                        Toast.LENGTH_LONG).show();
                return true;
            case 3:
                Toast.makeText(this, "You clicked on Item 4",
```

```
                           Toast.LENGTH_LONG).show();
                    return true;
               case 4:
                    Toast.makeText(this, "You clicked on Item 5",
                              Toast.LENGTH_LONG).show();
                    return true;
               case 5:
                    Toast.makeText(this, "You clicked on Item 6",
                              Toast.LENGTH_LONG).show();
                    return true;
               case 6:
                    Toast.makeText(this, "You clicked on Item 7",
                              Toast.LENGTH_LONG).show();
                    return true;
          }
          return false;
     }
}
```

Step 2: Run the application.

Run the application to view the screen in the emulator. Follow the below provided step-by-step instructions.

Click on the menu icon → Menu will be displayed → Click on menu item → "Item Selected" message will be shown. Refer to Figure 3-21.

Figure 3-21: Menu and menu item click events

List Views

Tutorial 4: Creating a List Views

In this tutorial, you will add a list view to your application. Implement the following business scenario.

Use Case Scenario:

- Add "Products" button to the main screen.
- Click on "Products" button → Display a list of products
- Click on "Product" → Show message
- Handle the list selection event and display a message on the screen.

The scenario described above is shown in Figure 3-22.

Figure 3-22: Working with list views

The steps required to implement the above-specified business scenario in Android are listed below:

1. Update main activity layout file.
2. Update the main activity class.
3. Add product activity class.
4. Add activity to your application manifest file.
5. Run the application.

The steps specified above are described in the following sections.

Step 1: Update the main activity layout file

Here, reuse the previously created "activity_main.xml" layout file. Add a new "Products" button to the main screen.

Go to res → layouts → Open "activity_main.xml" file. Add the button element provided below to the "activity_main.xml" file.

```
<Button
    android:id="@+id/products_button"
    android:layout_width="match_parent"
    android:layout_height="wrap_content"
    android:layout_marginBottom="5sp"
    android:layout_marginLeft="12dp"
    android:layout_marginRight="12dp"
    android:enabled="true"
    android:text="Products"
    android:onClick="CallProducts"
    android:textSize="30sp" />
```

The "android:onClick" attribute handles the button-click event.

Step 2: Update the main activity class

Here, reuse the previously created `MainActivity.java` class. Add the button-click event method for the "Products" button.

Go to java → Your package → Open "MainActivity.java" file. Add the event handling method provided below to the main activity class.

```
public void CallProducts(View view) {
    Intent intent = new Intent(this, ProductActivity.class);
    startActivity(intent);
}
```

The `CallProducts(...)` method invokes the product activity, which displays the list of products. The `Intent` class is used to invoke the other activity classes.

Step 3: Add product activity class

Add the `ProductActivity.java` class. This class must extend the `ListActivity` class. An example use is provided below.

```
public class ProductActivity extends ListActivity {
    ...
}
```

The `onListItemClick(...)` method handles list item click events.

Go to app → Java → Your package → Create `ProductActivity.java` class. This class is used to display the list of products.

Listing 3-3 provides the complete code for the product activity class.

Listing 3-3: ProductActivity.java class.

```java
package com.learning.android.androidbasics;

import android.app.ListActivity;
import android.os.Bundle;
import android.view.View;
import android.widget.ArrayAdapter;
import android.widget.ListView;
import android.widget.Toast;

// ProductActivity.java
public class ProductActivity extends ListActivity {

    private String listData[] = {"Product 1", "Product 2", "Product 3",
                                 "Product 4", "Product 5", "Product 6"};

    @Override
    protected void onCreate(Bundle savedInstanceState) {
        super.onCreate(savedInstanceState);

        ListView lstView = getListView();
        lstView.setChoiceMode(ListView.CHOICE_MODE_MULTIPLE);
        lstView.setTextFilterEnabled(true);

        setListAdapter(new ArrayAdapter<String>
            (this, android.R.layout.simple_list_item_1, listData));
    }

    public void onListItemClick(ListView parent, View v,
            int position, long id) {
        Toast.makeText(this, "You have selected " + listData[position],
                Toast.LENGTH_SHORT).show();
    }
}
```

Step 4: Add the activity to your application manifest file.

Don't forgot to add your activity class to the application manifest file. Open → manifests → AndroidManifest.xml file. Add the product activity.

```xml
<activity android:name=".ProductActivity"/>
```

Make sure, you have the dot (".") before the product activity class.

Step 5: Run the application

Follow the step-by-step instructions provided below to test the application.

1. Start the emulator
2. Main screen will be shown with "Products" button.
3. Click on "Products" button.
4. The application will invoke the product activity and displays the list of products (Refer to Figure 3-23).
5. Click on each product to view the message on screen.

Figure 3-23: Menu and menu item click events

Activities and Intents

Tutorial 5: Using Activities and Intents

This tutorial will help you to understand the use of activities and intents in Android application development. Two activities are communicated through intents; this is how we implement navigation in Android application development.

In this tutorial, you will add a product details screen to your application. Implement the following business scenario.

Use Case Scenario:

- Click on "Products" button on main screen → Display list of products
- Click on "Product" → Show product details
- Handle list selection event to show the product details screen.

The scenario described above is shown in Figure 3-24.

Figure 3-24: Working with list view and details

The steps required to implement the above-specified business scenario in Android are listed below:

1. Create the product details activity layout file.
2. Add the product details activity class.
3. Update the product activity class.
4. Add product details to your application manifest file.
5. Run the application.

The above-specified steps are described in the following sections:

Step 1: Create the product details activity class

Go to res → layouts → Create "activity_product_details.xml" file. This file contains two text fields; one for displays the product name, and the other displays the product details.

The complete XML file for the product details activity layout is provided below.

```
<RelativeLayout xmlns:android=
    "http://schemas.android.com/apk/res/android"
    xmlns:tools="http://schemas.android.com/tools"
    android:layout_width="match_parent"
    android:layout_height="match_parent"
    android:paddingBottom="@dimen/activity_vertical_margin"
    android:paddingLeft="@dimen/activity_horizontal_margin"
    android:paddingRight="@dimen/activity_horizontal_margin"
    android:paddingTop="@dimen/activity_vertical_margin">

    <LinearLayout
        android:layout_width="match_parent"
```

```
            android:layout_height="wrap_content"
            android:layout_gravity="center_horizontal"
            android:orientation="vertical">

        <TextView
            android:id="@+id/product_name"
            android:layout_width="match_parent"
            android:layout_height="wrap_content"
            android:layout_marginTop="5dp"
            android:enabled="true"
            android:text=""
            android:textColor="#ff000000"
            android:textSize="25dp" />

        <TextView
            android:id="@+id/product_details"
            android:layout_width="match_parent"
            android:layout_height="wrap_content"
            android:layout_marginTop="5dp"
            android:enabled="true"
            android:text=""
            android:textColor="#ff000000" />

    </LinearLayout>

</RelativeLayout>
```

Step 2: Add the product details activity class.

In this step, you will create the product details activity class. This class renders the previously created "activity_product_details.xml" layout file. This class receives the selected product, and displays the details of the product.

Go to app → Java → Your package → Create `ProductDetailsActivity.java` class. This class provide the details of the product.

Listing 3-4 provides the complete code for the product details activity class.

Listing 3-4: ProductDetailsActivity.java class.

```
package com.learning.android.androidbasics;

import android.app.Activity;
import android.os.Bundle;
import android.widget.Button;
import android.widget.TextView;

// ProductDetailsActivity.java
public class ProductDetailsActivity extends Activity {

    @Override
    protected void onCreate(Bundle savedInstanceState) {
        super.onCreate(savedInstanceState);
        setContentView(R.layout.activity_product_details);

        // Receiving the selected product
```

```
String productName = getIntent().getStringExtra("productName");

TextView productNameView = (TextView)
            findViewById(R.id.product_name);
productNameView.setText(productName);

TextView detailsView = (TextView)
            findViewById(R.id.product_details);
detailsView.setText("Vector calculus  is a branch of
            mathematics concerned with differentiation
            and integration ");
    }
}
```

Step 3: Update the product activity class.

Here, reuse the previously created `ProductActivity` class. Update the `onListItemClick(...)` method. We will use the `putExtra(...)` method to pass the data from one activity to another. An example code is provided below.

```
intent.putExtra("productName", listData[position]);
```

The complete method code is provided below.

```
public void onListItemClick(ListView parent, View v,
                int position, long id) {
    Intent intent = new Intent(this, ProductDetailsActivity.class);

    // Passing data from product activity to product details activity
    intent.putExtra("productName", listData[position]);
    startActivity(intent);
}
```

Step 4: Add the product details to your application manifest file

Don't forgot to add your activity class to the application manifest file. Open → manifests → "AndroidManifest.xml" file. Add the product details activity.

```
<activity android:name=".ProductDetailsActivity"/>
```

Step 5: Run the application.

Follow the step-by-step instructions provided below to test the application.

1. Start the emulator.
2. Main screen will be shown with "Products" button.
3. Click on the "Products" button.
4. The application will invoke the product activity and displays the list of products (Refer to Figure 3-24)
5. Click on each product.
6. The product details screen will be displayed.

Progress Dialog Spinner

Tutorial 6: Implementing Progress Dialog Spinner

This tutorial will help you to learn about the progress dialog spinner. The spinner shows the progress of the operations that take long time to execute. Android's `ProgressDialog` class is used to show progress dialogs.

The following code shows the progress bar.

```
progressBar.show();
```

The following code hides the progress bar.

```
progressBar.hide();
```

The following code kills the progress bar.

```
progressBar.dismiss();
```

An example code is provided below.

```
ProgressDialog progressBar = new ProgressDialog(v.getContext());
progressBar.setCancelable(true);
progressBar.setMessage("Processing ...");
progressBar.setProgressStyle(ProgressDialog.STYLE_SPINNER);
progressBar.setProgress(0);
progressBar.setMax(100);
progressBar.show();
```

Implement the following business scenario.

Use Case Scenario:

- Click on "Products" button on main screen → Display list of products
- Click on "Product" → View the progress dialog for some time → Show the product details screen.

The scenario described above is shown in Figure 3-25.

The steps required to implement the above-specified scenario in Android are listed below:

1. Update the product activity class
2. Run the application

These steps are described in the following sections:

Figure 3-25: Progress dialog spinner.

Step 1: Update product activity class

Here, reuse the previously created `ProductActivity` class, updating the `onListItemClick(...)` method.

```
public void onListItemClick(ListView parent, View v,
                int position, long id) {

    ProgressDialog progressBar = new ProgressDialog(v.getContext());
    progressBar.setCancelable(true);
    progressBar.setMessage("Processing ...");
    progressBar.setProgressStyle(ProgressDialog.STYLE_SPINNER);
    progressBar.setProgress(0);
    progressBar.setMax(100);
    progressBar.show();

    try {
        Thread.sleep(900);
    } catch (Exception ex) {
        ex.printStackTrace();
    }

    Intent intent = new Intent(this, ProductDetailsActivity.class);
    intent.putExtra("productName", listData[position]);
    startActivity(intent);
}
```

Step 2: Run the application

Run the application to view the progress bar as shown in Figure 3-25.

Tutorial 7: Programmatically Creating a User Interface

In Android, we can use the two approaches for creating a user interface.

1. Using XML layout files
2. Using Android API.

This tutorial will show you how to create a user interface programmatically using Android API. The following code is used for creating a linear layout with vertical orientation.

```
LinearLayout layout = new LinearLayout(this);
layout.setOrientation(LinearLayout.VERTICAL);
```

Use following code to create a text view (label).

```
TextView tv = new TextView(this);
```

Use the following code to creates an edit text view

```
EditText et = new EditText(this);
```

Use the following code to create a button view

```
Button btn = new Button(this);
```

Listing 3-5 provides the complete activity class code. Note the inline comments provided in the code.

Listing 3-5: DynamicUIActivity.java class.

```
package com.example.andriodlearning;

import android.app.Activity;
import android.graphics.Color;
import android.os.Bundle;
import android.text.Editable;
import android.view.View;
import android.widget.Button;
import android.widget.EditText;
import android.widget.LinearLayout;
import android.view.ViewGroup.LayoutParams;
import android.widget.TextView;
import android.widget.Toast;

// DynamicUIActivity.java
public class DynamicUIActivity extends Activity {

    private EditText et;

    @Override
    protected void onCreate(Bundle savedInstanceState) {
        super.onCreate(savedInstanceState);

        LayoutParams params = new LinearLayout.LayoutParams(
```

```java
            LayoutParams.MATCH_PARENT,
            LayoutParams.WRAP_CONTENT);

    // Creating linear layout
    LinearLayout layout = new LinearLayout(this);
    layout.setOrientation(LinearLayout.VERTICAL);

    // Creating a textview
    TextView tv = new TextView(this);
    tv.setText("Comments:");
    tv.setLayoutParams(params);
    tv.setEnabled(true);
    tv.setTextSize(25.00f);
    tv.setBackgroundColor(Color.WHITE);

    // Creating a edit text
    et = new EditText(this);
    et.setTextSize(25.0f);
    et.setEnabled(true);
    et.setBackgroundColor(Color.GRAY);
    et.setLayoutParams(params);
    et.setHint("Please enter comments");
    et.setHintTextColor(Color.RED);

    // Creating a button
    Button btn = new Button(this);
    btn.setText("Save");
    btn.setLayoutParams(params);
    btn.setEnabled(true);
    btn.setTextSize(20.00f);

    // Adding the textview
    layout.addView(tv);

    // Adding the Edit Field
    layout.addView(et);

    // Adding the button
    layout.addView(btn);

    // Creating a layout parameters for the layout
    LinearLayout.LayoutParams layoutParam = new
            LinearLayout.LayoutParams(
            LayoutParams.MATCH_PARENT,
            LayoutParams.WRAP_CONTENT);

    // Rendering the layout
    this.addContentView(layout, layoutParam);

    // Handling Save click action
    btn.setOnClickListener(saveButtonListener);
}

// Receiving Save button click action
private View.OnClickListener saveButtonListener = new
View.OnClickListener() {
    public void onClick(View v) {
```

```
                    Toast.makeText(getBaseContext(), ((Button) v).getText() + "
                    was clicked", Toast.LENGTH_LONG).show();

                    // Click on Save button
                    Editable comments = (Editable) et.getText();
                    String commentsStr = comments.toString().trim();
                    Toast.makeText(getBaseContext(), commentsStr,
                            Toast.LENGTH_LONG).show();
            }
        };
}
```

Figure 3-26 shows the output of the above activity.

Figure 3-26 creating user interface programmatically.

Alert Dialog

This tutorial will help you to learn the Alert Dialogs in Android application development. Display alert dialog to obtain user conformation.

The following code creates an alert dialog.

```
AlertDialog.Builder alertDialogBuilder = new AlertDialog.Builder(this);
```

The following code shows an alert dialog.

```
AlertDialog alertDialog = alertDialogBuilder.create();
alertDialog.show();
```

The following code closes an alert dialog.

```
dialogInterface.cancel();
```

The following code sets a title to an alert window.

```
alertDialogBuilder.setTitle("Make a Decision");
```

The following code shows an alert message.

```
alertDialogBuilder.setMessage("Did you make the Decision ?");
```

Figure 3-27 Alert dialog

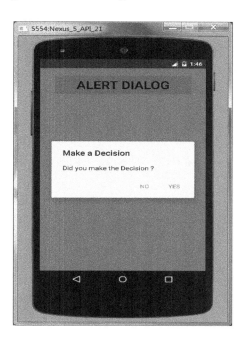

The complete alert dialog code is provided below. Note the code inline comments.

```
public void showAlertDialog(View view) {
    AlertDialog.Builder alertDialogBuilder = new
                    AlertDialog.Builder(this);

    // Setting alert title
    alertDialogBuilder.setTitle("Make a Decision");

    // Setting alert message
    alertDialogBuilder.setMessage("Did you make the Decision ?");

    alertDialogBuilder.setPositiveButton("Yes", new
                DialogInterface.OnClickListener() {
        @Override
        public void onClick(DialogInterface dialogIf, int id) {
            // Yes button is clicked
            Toast.makeText(MainActivity.this, "YES is clicked",
                    Toast.LENGTH_LONG).show();
        }
    });

    alertDialogBuilder.setNegativeButton("No", new
```

```
            DialogInterface.OnClickListener() {
        @Override
        public void onClick(DialogInterface dialog, int id) {
            // "No" button is clicked
            dialog.cancel();
        }
    });

    // Show an alert dialog
    AlertDialog alertDialog = alertDialogBuilder.create();
    alertDialog.show();
}
```

The output of the above method is shown in Figure 3-27.

Summary

This section summarizes the commonly used terminology in Android application development. Figure 3-28 summarizes the most important points described in this chapter.

Figure 3-28 Android widgets

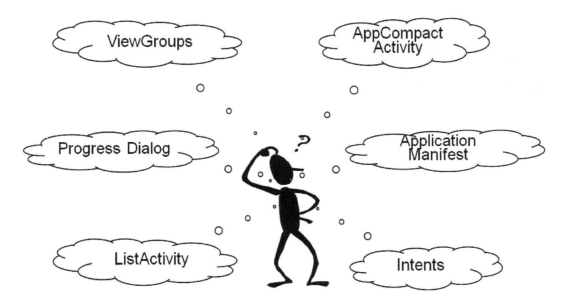

- The `Intent` class is used to invoke an activity from other activity class. The intents `putExtra(...)` method is used to pass data from one activity to another activity.
- The `ProgressDialog` class is used to show Android progress dialogs for operations that take long time to execute.
- A view group/layout can contain a collection of views (UI elements). Each view group arranges the views in a specific format.
- The `ListActivity` class is used to render and display collections data in a list format.
- The `AppCompactActivity` class is used to inflate the menus and handle the menu click events.

- The Android application manifest file contains all your application activities, themes, and styles.

Chapter 4. Android Frameworks

Android developers can use various open-source frameworks in application development. These frameworks simplify the application development in Android. This chapter illustrates the use of various available open-source frameworks in Android application development. The commonly used Android application development frameworks are listed below.

- Spring Android
- Dagger
- Event Bus
- Picasso
- XML Parsing

This chapter will discuss the following topics:

- Using Android frameworks in application development.
- How to invoke REST-based web services using the Spring Android framework.
- How to implement dependency injection using the Dagger framework.
- How to use the Event Bus framework in application development
- How to use the Picasso for loading, caching, and transforming images.
- How to build and parse XML in Android.

Anatomy of Android Frameworks

Spring Android

The phrase "Spring Framework" has been a box-office hit for several years. Enterprise applications have been using the Spring framework for more than a decade. It is an open-source application framework and Inversion of Control (IOC) container for the Java platform. Rod Johnson invented this framework in 2002, and it was released under the Apache license in 2003.

The Spring framework provides several modules for developing enterprise applications. Spring framework modules can also be integrated with other software components. The services provided by each module can be used at various layers for developing enterprise applications. Applications can take advantage of these services for developing enterprise applications. The spring framework is very popular in the Java community, and has become an integral part of the application development for Java-based applications.

Spring Android is an extension of the Spring project. The framework provides an API to access REST-based web services in Android applications. Spring Android is a tiny, light-weight project. It does not provide any dependency injection (DI) or inversion of control (IOC) capabilities for Android platform. Spring Android provides the following features.

- A REST client for accessing REST-based web services.
- OAuth API's for connecting to social media.

The Spring-provided `RestTemplate` class is used to invoke REST-based Web service endpoints. The code provided below illustrates the use of the `RestTemplate` class.

In the following example, the client is passing a single parameter to invoke the REST service.

```
RestTemplate restTemplate = new RestTemplate();
String requestURL1 = "http://localhost:8080/wsbook/
                        services/gradeservice/grade/{grade}";
String result = restTemplate.getForObject(
                requestURL1, String.class, "1");
```

In the following example, the client is passing multiple parameters to invoke the REST service.

```
Map<String, String> vars = new HashMap<String, String>();
vars.put("grade", "1");
vars.put("subject", "Java");

String requestURL2 = "http://localhost:8080/wsbook/services/gradeservice/
                        grade/{grade}/subject/{subject}";
String result1= restTemplate.getForObject(requestURL2,String.class,vars);
```

In the following example, the client is passing multiple parameters to invoke the REST service.

```
Map<String, String> topics = new HashMap<String, String>();
vars.put("grade", "1");
vars.put("subject", "Math");
vars.put("topic", "Mathematics and art");

String requestURL3 = "http://localhost:8080/wsbook/services/gradeservice/
                grade/1/subject/{subject}/topic/{topic}";
String result2= restTemplate.getForObject(requestURL3,
                                    String.class, topics);
```

NOTE: Tutorial -1 provides the complete details on implementing the Spring Android framework

---

Event Bus

Event Bus is a publish-subscribe messaging model for Android. Messaging is a method of loosely coupled communication between two applications or software components. Green Robot event bus is an open-source project which provides a simplified messaging model for Android.

The Event Bus publish-subscribe messaging model has the following characteristics.

- Commonly used terminology in the Event Bus publish-subscribe messaging model: publisher, subscriber, event, and post. The message producer is called the publisher; the message consumer is called the subscriber.
- The publisher post's an event to the Event Bus; Subscribers receive the events. Depending on the event type, the subscriber's `onEvent()` method will be invoked automatically.
- The publish-subscribe messaging model is equivalent to an observer design pattern (GOF design pattern)

The publish-subscribe messaging model is shown in Figure 4-1.

Figure 4-1: Publish-subscribe messaging model

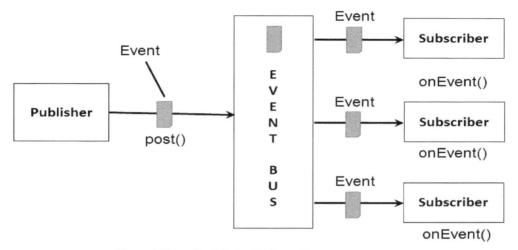

Event Bus Publish-Subscribe messaging

NOTE: Tutorial -2 provides the complete details on implementing the Event bus model.

Dagger

Dagger is a dependency injection framework for Android. The process of defining the objects, configuring the objects and their dependencies, and injecting the bean references into their dependent objects is called "dependency injection (DI)". The Dagger API can be used to inject those dependencies while creating the bean instances. Dagger provides a simple light-weight dependency injection framework for Android.

The following example illustrates the use of Dagger API. The `Motor` referenced below has both getter and setter methods.

```
package com.example.androidlearning.dagger;

public class Motor {
    ...
}
```

The below provided `Vehicle` class has a reference to the `Motor` class. The instance of the `Motor` class object is injected into the `Vehicle` class constructor. The `@Inject` annotation is used to inject the `Motor` class object into the `Vehicle` class. See the example below.

```
package com.example.androidlearning.dagger;

public class Vehicle {

    private Motor motor;
```

```
        @Inject
        public Vehicle(Motor motor){
            this.motor = motor;
        }
}
```

NOTE: This book does not cover dependency injection or IOC topics. Refer to authors *Spring Framework* book for more information. Tutorial -4 provides the complete details on implementing the dependency injection using Dagger.

Picasso

Picasso provides an API for loading, caching, and transforming images. The following code loads an image.

```
Picasso.with(this).load(R.drawable.apple).into(imageView);
```

Similarly, the following code resizes an image.

```
Picasso.with(this).load(R.drawable.apple)
                  .resize(250, 200)
                  .rotate(90)
                  .into(imageView2);
```

NOTE: Tutorial -4 provides the complete details for implementing Picasso

---

XML Parsing

Let's review a simple XML document containing three elements: id, first name, and last name.

```
<?xml version="1.0" encoding="UTF-8"?>
<Students>
    <Student>
        <id>1</id>
        <firstName>John</firstName>
        <lastName>Smith</lastName>
    </Student>
</Students>
```

How do you read the element data from the above XML? The data specified in XML is "id" (value =1), "firstName" (value = John) and "lastName" (value = Smith).

The objective here is to read the data from an XML document and populate the values into the appropriate Java class. The equivalent Java object used to populate the above-specified XML data is given below. The input is an XML document, and the output will be a Java object populated with data.

```
public class Student {
    private String id;
    private String firstName;
```

```
        private String lastName;

        // Add getters and setters here
}
```

What are the possible ways to read the data from an XML document? The possible solutions are given below.

- Load the entire document, store it in your system memory, and then access the required element data using the Java API.
- Read only the required portions of an XML document based on a generated event. Each generated event should map to a specific portion of the XML document. From a generated event you can either pull the data from an XML document or ask the XML document to push the data for a generated event using Java API.

A couple of solutions are available to us for reading the data from XML documents. Now the question is how to create (write) an XML document. In this scenario, the input is a Java object containing data; and the output will be an XML document. The input Java object with hard-coded data is given below.

```
public class Student {
        private String id = "823147";
        private String firstName = "John";
        private String lastName = "Smith";

        // Add getters and setters
}
```

The output is an XML document.

```
<?xml version="1.0" encoding="UTF-8"?>
<Students>
        <Student>
                <id>823147</id>
                <firstName>John</firstName>
                <lastName>Smith</lastName>
        </Student>
</Students>
```

We have Java-based APIs available to create an XML document. The technique used for reading and writing XML documents is called Java API for XML processing; it is also called JAXP.

Java API for XML processing (JAXP) is a Java specification that introduces support for creating, manipulating, validating, and parsing XML documents using standardized Java APIs. XML is the most commonly used language in Web services, so it is necessary to understand XML processing, creation, validation, and manipulation techniques. This chapter does not address basic XML syntax or rules. The three basic JAXP-provided interfaces used for this purpose are given below.

- Simple API for XML (called SAX)
- Document Object Model (called DOM)
- Streaming API for XML (called StAX)

SAX is used for reading XML documents; DOM and StAX are used for both reading and writing XML documents. SAX, DOM, and StAX all are part of Java SE. The "javax.xml" package provides classes and interfaces for processing XML documents.

The Android platform can use JAXP API's for XML processing. JAXP is part of JDK. Also, the latest JDK provides an annotation-based programming model.

Simple XML

Simple XML is an open-source XML framework, which can be used for processing XML in Android. This chapter will help you to understand the annotations provided with Simple XML and how to use them. The following annotations are illustrated in this section.

- @Root
- @Element
- @ElementList
- @Attribute

@Root

The @Root annotation is used with top-level class or enum types. The following example demonstrates the use of the @Root annotation. The class Products is annotated with the following parameter values.

```
@Root(name="employees")
public class Products implements Serializable {
    ...

    // Add getters and setters
}
```

The resulting XML is:

```
<?xml version="1.0" encoding="UTF-8" standalone="yes"?>
<products>
    <!-- Creats outer element, enclose other elements to this -->
</products>
```

@Element

The @Element annotation is used with Java bean properties and class-level fields. The following example demonstrates the use of the @Element annotation.

```
@Root
public class Products implements Serializable {

    @Element(name = "firstName")
    private String firstName;
```

```
    // Add getters and setters
}
```

The resulting XML is:

```
<?xml version="1.0" encoding="UTF-8" standalone="yes"?>
<products>
    <firstName> ... </firstName>
</products>
```

@ElementList

The `@Element` annotation is used with Java bean properties to enclose the list of elements. The following example demonstrates the use of the `@ElementList` annotation.

```
@Root
public class Products implements Serializable {

    @ElementList(inline=true)
    private List<Product> productList;

    // Add getters and setters
}
```

The resulting XML is:

```
<?xml version="1.0" encoding="UTF-8" standalone="yes"?>
<products>
    <product>
        ...
    </product>

    <product>
        ...
    </product>
</products>
```

@Attribute

The `@Attribute` annotation is used with Java bean properties to specify the XML attributes. The following example demonstrates the use of the `@Attribute` annotation.

```
@Element(name="product")
public class Product implements Serializable {

    @Attribute
    public String id;

    @Attribute
    public String href;

    // Add getters and setters
```

```
}
```

The resulting XML is:

```
<product id="209277" href="http:/localhost:8080/myservice/productId/277">
    ...
</product>
```

To use the Simple XML framework in your application, add the following dependencies to your "build.gradle" file.

```
compile('org.simpleframework:simple-xml:2.7.1') {
    exclude group: 'stax', module: 'stax-api'
    exclude group: 'xpp3', module: 'xpp3'
}
```

NOTE: Tutorial -1 provides the complete details for implementing Simple XML. This book does not cover JAXP or XML.

AsyncTask

Android provides the `AsyncTasc` class, which allows you to run tasks in background. It supports both serial and parallel execution of tasks.

The following method is used to execute tasks one at a time (i.e., serially).

```
execute(...);
```

The following method is used to execute tasks in parallel.

```
executeOnExecutor(...);
```

The asynchronous task uses the following callback methods.

- `onPreExecute(...)`
- `doInBackground(...)`
- `onProgressUpdate(...)`
- `onPostExecute(...)`

The `onPreExecute(...)` method is invoked before the task is executed. This method is used to show the things to the user while executing an operation in background. For example: you might show the user a progress bar while the operation is executing. An example code is provided below.

```
protected Map<String, String> doInBackground(Void... params) {
    ...
}
```

The `doInBackground(...)` method is invoked immediately after the task finishes executing the `onPreExecute(...)` method. This method is used to invoke the actual operation that takes a long time to execute. See the sample code below.

```
@Override
protected Map<String, String> doInBackground(Void... params) {
    // Invoking a web service endpoint
    Map<String, String> namesMap = invokeRestService();
    return namesMap;
}
```

The actual timing of the `onProgressUpdate(...)` method is undefined. This method is used to update the things while a long-executing operation is in progress. For example, use this method to update the progress bar, or change the progress bar spinner. See the sample code below.

```
@Override
protected void onProgressUpdate(Void... values) {
    ...
}
```

The `onPostExecute(...)` method is executed on the thread after the background process operation is completed. The output of the `doInBackground(...)` method is passed as a paramter to this method. See the sample code below.

```
@Override
protected void onPostExecute(Map<String, String> result) {
    Status status = getStatus();
    ...
}
```

The following points illustrates the usage of the `AsyncTask` class.

- The `AsyncTask` class must be subclassed to use.
- The `AsyncTask` must override at least the `doInBackground(...)` method.
- Return type of `doInBackground(...)` must match the `onPostExecute(...)` method parameter.
- Methods `onPostExecute()`, `onPreExecute()`, and `onProgressUpdate()` should not be explicitly called.

An example use of a sub-classed `AsyncTask` is provided below.

```
public class RestServiceClient extends
            AsyncTask<Void, Void, Map<String, String>> {
    ...
}
```

NOTE: Tutorial -1 provides the details on implementing `AsyncTask`

Why do we need AsyncTask?

In Web applications, it is possible to invoke the external SOAP and REST-based Web services synchronously from the application. This approach is not allowed in the mobile development. Time consuming operations and external Web services will be invoked asynchronously using `AsyncTask` class. This class allows you to execute the tasks in background, and it supports both serial and parallel execution.

Spring Android

Tutorial 1: Invoking REST service endpoints

The following business scenario is implemented using Spring Android.

Use Case Scenario:

- Design a main screen with "Spring REST" button.
- Click on "Spring REST" button. User navigates to the next screen, which shows "First Name" and "Last Name"
- Invoke the REST web service asynchronously. Assuming REST service returns the XML/JSON data.
- Do the XML to Object conversion, display the output on screen.

The above described navigation scenario is shown in Figure 4-2.

Figure 4-2: Main and navigation screens

The steps required to implement the above-specified business scenario in Android using `AsyncTask` class are listed below:

---

1. Work on your configurations
2. Create a main layout file.
3. Create spring layout file.
4. Create Activity classes
5. Create POJO classes
6. Create a REST helper class
7. Test the application.

The above-specified steps are described in the following sections:

Step 1: Work on your configurations

The following configurations are required to make Sprind-Android to work. Add required spring dependencies to "build.gradle" file. The required dependencies are provided below.

```
// Added due to Spring modules
packagingOptions {
    exclude 'META-INF/DEPENDENCIES'
    exclude 'META-INF/notice'
    exclude 'META-INF/license'
    exclude 'META-INF/notice.txt'
    exclude 'META-INF/license.txt'
    exclude 'META-INF/ASL2.0'
}

// Spring dependencies - Adding spring REST module
compile 'org.springframework.android:spring-android-rest-
template:1.0.1.RELEASE'

// Spring dependencies - Adding spring android core module
compile 'org.springframework.android:spring-android-core'

// Spring dependencies - Used for XML to Object conversions
compile('org.simpleframework:simple-xml:2.7.1') {
        exclude group: 'stax', module: 'stax-api'
        exclude group: 'xpp3', module: 'xpp3'
}
```

Add the following configurations to "androidmanifest.xml" file. These configurations are required for accessing web services deployed outside your network.

```
<uses-permission android:name="android.permission.INTERNET"/>
<uses-permission android:name="android.permission.ACCESS_WIFI_STATE"/>
<uses-permission android:name="android.permission.CHANGE_WIFI_STATE"/>
<uses-permission android:name="android.permission.CHANGE_NETWORK_STATE"/>
<uses-permission android:name="android.permission.ACCESS_NETWORK_STATE"/>
```

Step 2: Create a main layout file.

Go to res → layout → create "activity_main.xml" layout file. The following "activity_main.xml" file is used to create the main screen.

```
<RelativeLayout xmlns:android =
    "http://schemas.android.com/apk/res/android"
    xmlns:tools="http://schemas.android.com/tools"
```

```
        android:layout_width="match_parent"
        android:layout_height="match_parent"
        android:paddingLeft="@dimen/activity_horizontal_margin"
        android:paddingRight="@dimen/activity_horizontal_margin"
        android:paddingTop="@dimen/activity_vertical_margin"
        android:paddingBottom="@dimen/activity_vertical_margin"
        tools:context=".MainActivity">

    <LinearLayout
        android:layout_width="match_parent"
        android:layout_height="wrap_content"
        android:layout_gravity="center_horizontal"
        android:orientation="vertical">

        <Button
            android:id="@+id/spring_button"
            android:layout_width="250dp"
            android:layout_height="wrap_content"
            android:layout_marginBottom="5sp"
            android:layout_marginLeft="60dp"
            android:layout_marginRight="12dp"
            android:enabled="true"
            android:text="Spring REST"
            android:textSize="30sp"/>

    </LinearLayout>
</RelativeLayout>
```

Step 3: Create spring layout file.

Go to res → layout → create "activity_spring.xml" layout file.

The following "activity_spring.xml" file is used to create the navigation screen. This layout displays the user specific attributes such as first name, last name, products, and so forth.

```
<?xml version="1.0" encoding="utf-8"?>
<LinearLayout xmlns:android="http://schemas.android.com/apk/res/android"
    android:layout_width="fill_parent"
    android:layout_height="fill_parent"
    android:orientation="vertical">

    <TextView
        android:text="First Name"
        android:layout_marginTop="5dp"
        android:enabled="true"
        android:layout_width="match_parent"
        android:layout_height="wrap_content"/>

    <EditText
        android:id="@+id/firstName"
        android:textSize="30sp"
        android:layout_marginTop="5dp"
        android:enabled="true"
        android:layout_width="match_parent"
        android:layout_height="wrap_content"/>
```

```xml
    <TextView
        android:text="Last Name"
        android:layout_marginTop="5dp"
        android:enabled="true"
        android:layout_width="match_parent"
        android:layout_height="wrap_content"/>

    <EditText
        android:id="@+id/lastName"
        android:textSize="30sp"
        android:layout_marginTop="5dp"
        android:enabled="true"
        android:layout_width="match_parent"
        android:layout_height="wrap_content"/>

</LinearLayout>
```

Step 4: Create activity classes.

The following `MainActivity.java` class is used to create main screen with "Spring REST" button. This activity class renders the previously created "activity_main.xml" layout file.

Listing 4-1 provides the main activity class. Note the code inline comments.

Listing 4-1: MainActivity.java class.

```java
package com.example.androidlearning;

import android.app.Activity;
import android.content.Intent;
import android.os.Bundle;
import android.view.Menu;
import android.view.MenuItem;
import android.view.View;
import android.widget.Button;

import com.example.androidlearning.db.SQLiteActivity;

// MainActivity.java
public class MainActivity extends Activity {

    @Override
    protected void onCreate(Bundle savedInstanceState) {
        super.onCreate(savedInstanceState);
        setContentView(R.layout.activity_main);

        // Button event listener to capture the click event
        Button springButton =(Button) findViewById(R.id.spring_button);
        springButton.setEnabled(true);
        springButton.setOnClickListener(springButtonListener);
    }

    // Create an anonymous class to act as a button click listener
    private View.OnClickListener springButtonListener = new
    View.OnClickListener() {
        public void onClick(View v) {
            callSpringRestService();
```

```
            }
        };

        // Navigating to user data scren
        private void callSpringRestService() {
            Intent intent = new Intent(this, SpringActivity.class);
            startActivity(intent);
        }
    }
```

The following `SpringActivity.java` class is used to create the user data screen with "First Name" and "Last Name" elements. This class renders the previously created layout "activity_spring.xml" file.

Listing 4-2 provides the Spring activity class. Note the code inline comments.

Listing 4-2: SpringActivity.java class.

```
package com.example.androidlearning.spring;

import android.app.Activity;
import android.os.Bundle;
import android.util.Log;
import android.widget.EditText;
import com.example.androidlearning.R;

// SpringActivity.java
public class SpringActivity extends Activity {

    @Override
    protected void onCreate(Bundle savedInstanceState) {
        super.onCreate(savedInstanceState);
        setContentView(R.layout.activity_spring);

        EditText firstName = (EditText) findViewById(R.id.firstName);
        EditText lastName = (EditText) findViewById(R.id.lastName);

        // Calling the REST service Asynchronously
        RestServiceClient restClient =
            new RestServiceClient(firstName, lastName);
        restClient.execute();
    }

    @Override
    // Called when the activity becomes visible to the user
    protected void onStart() {
        super.onStart();
    }

    @Override
    // Called when the activity is no longer visible to the user
    protected void onStop() {
        super.onStop();
    }
}
```

Step 5: Create POJO classes.

The following POJO class is used to store the product-specific details such as name, description, and so forth.

```
package com.example.androidlearning.spring;

import org.simpleframework.xml.Attribute;
import org.simpleframework.xml.Element;
import java.io.Serializable;

@Element(name="product")
public class Product implements Serializable {

    @Element
    private String name;

    @Element
    private String shortDescription;

    @Element
    private String longDescription;

    @Attribute
    public String id;

    @Attribute
    public String href;

    // Add getter and setter methods
}
```

The following POJO class is used to store the name and product information. This class generates the XML root element.

```
package com.example.androidlearning.spring;

import org.simpleframework.xml.Element;
import org.simpleframework.xml.ElementList;
import org.simpleframework.xml.Root;

import java.io.Serializable;
import java.util.List;

@Root
public class Products implements Serializable {

    @Element(name = "firstName")
    private String firstName;

    @Element(name = "lastName")
    private String lastName;

    @ElementList(inline=true)
    private List<Product> productList;
```

```
        // Add getter and setter methods
}
```

Step 6: Create REST helper classes.

The following `RestServiceClient` helper class is used to invoke the REST-based Web service endpoint. This class must follow the below specified rules.

- `RestServiceClient` class must extend the `AsyncTask`.
- Spring-provided `RestTemplate` class is used to invoke the REST-based web service endpoint
- The life cycle methods `onPostExecute()`, `onPreExecute()`, and `onProgressUpdate()` should not be explicitly called.

Listing 4-3 provides the complete class code. Note the code inline comments.

Listing 4-3: RestServiceClient.java class.

```java
package com.example.androidlearning.spring;

import android.os.AsyncTask;
import android.util.Log;
import android.widget.EditText;

import org.simpleframework.xml.Serializer;
import org.simpleframework.xml.core.Persister;
import org.springframework.http.converter.StringHttpMessageConverter;
import org.springframework.web.client.RestTemplate;

import java.io.*;
import java.net.Authenticator;
import java.net.HttpURLConnection;
import java.net.URL;
import java.util.*;

// RestServiceClient.java
public class RestServiceClient extends
        AsyncTask<Void, Void, Map<String, String>> {

    private EditText firstName;
    private EditText lastName;

    public RestServiceClient(EditText firstName, EditText lastName) {
        this.firstName = firstName;
        this.lastName = lastName;
    }

    @Override
    protected Map<String, String> doInBackground(Void... params) {
        Map<String, String> namesMap = invokeRestService();
        return namesMap;
    }

    @Override
    protected void onPostExecute(Map<String, String> result) {
        // Execution of result of Long time consuming operation
```

```java
        // Printing the status of the thread
        Status status = getStatus();
        System.out.println("------ Status -----" + status.name());

        // Setting data to edit text fields
        firstName.setText(result.get("firstName"));
        lastName.setText(result.get("lastName"));
    }

    @Override
    protected void onPreExecute() {
        /* Things to be done before execution of long running
            operation. For example showing Progress Dialog. */
        System.out.println("------- onPreExecute --------");
    }

    @Override
    protected void onProgressUpdate(Void... values) {
        /* Things to be done while execution of long running operation
            is in progress. For example updating ProgessDialog */
        System.out.println("------ onProgressUpdate -----");
    }

    // This method invokes the REST service endpoint
    private Map<String, String> invokeRestService() {
        try {
            Authenticator.setDefault(new ProxyAuthenticator("fcwl",
                                        "3943Round#"));
            System.setProperty("http.proxyHost",
                        "in00pxy1.opr.statefarm.org");
            System.setProperty("http.proxyPort", "8000");

            /* Using Spring REST template class to invoke the REST
                services. */
            RestTemplate restTemplate = new RestTemplate();
            String url = "http://localhost:8080/myrestservice/userName/
                        jsmith/products";
            restTemplate.getMessageConverters().
                        add(new StringHttpMessageConverter());
            String xmlData =
                restTemplate.getForObject(url, String.class);

            Log.i("------ outputXML -----", xmlData);
            /* Converting XML to a Java object using Simple XML
                framework. */
            Serializer serializer = new Persister();
            Reader reader = new StringReader(xmlData);
            Products products = serializer.read(Products.class,
                        reader, false);

            // Printing the data.
            Log.i("------ First Name -----", products.getFirstName());
            Log.i("------ Last Name  -----", products.getLastName());
            List<Product> prodList = products.getProductList();
            for(Product product : prodList) {
                Log.i("------ Id -----", product.getId());
```

```
                    Log.i("------ Short Description -----",
                            product.getShortDescription());
                    Log.i("------ Long Description -----",
                            product.getLongDescription());
                    Log.i("------ Href -----", product.getHref());
            }

            // Building an output map data
            Map<String, String> namesMap=new HashMap<String, String>();
            namesMap.put("firstName", products.getFirstName());
            namesMap.put("lastName", products.getLastName());

            return namesMap;
        } catch (Exception ex) {
            ex.printStackTrace();
        }

        return null;
    }
}
```

Step 7: Structure of the REST output XML.

The structure of the REST service output is provided below. You can design your own XML to test the application.

```
<?xml version="1.0" encoding="UTF-8"?>
<products>
    <firstName>John</firstName>
    <lastName>Smith</lastName>
    <product id="209277"
        href="http:/localhost:8080/myrestservice/
                userName/jsmith/productId/209277">
        <name>Andorid Reference</name>
        <shortDescription>Android tutorial guide</shortDescription>
        <longDescription>Android tutorial guide</longDescription>
    </product>

    <product id="280957" href="http:/localhost:8080/myrestservice/
            userName/joewatson/productId/209277">
        <name>MyBatis Reference</name>
        <shortDescription>MyBatis in Practice</shortDescription>
        <longDescription>MyBatis in Practice</longDescription>
    </product>
</products>
```

Step 8: Test the application.

Follow the below provided step-by-step instructions to test the application.

1. Start the emulator
2. Click on application Icon → Main screen will be shown with "Spring REST" button.
3. Click on "Spring REST" button
4. The application will invoke the REST Web service endpoint. Displays the data on screen (Refer to Figure 4-2)

5. Only "First Name" and "Last Name" is displayed on user interface. View the console print statements for complete data.

Advantages

- Simple, tiny, and light-weight project
- Spring developers can reuse their skill in Android application development.
- We can reuse the same API in web and mobile development.
- Provides support for GET, POST, PUT, and DELERE operations.

Limitations

Spring framework is very popular in Java landscape. Spring Android is no way comparable with spring web application framework. Does not provide any dependency injection and IOC capabilities in Android.

When to use?

This Spring Android framework provides an API, to access the REST-based web services in Android applications. Consider this framework If you want to reuse the existing business logic in Android applications.

Event Bus

The following business scenario is implemented using Green Robot event bus.

Figure 4-3: Main and navigation screens

Use Case Scenario:

- Design a main screen with "Event Bus" button (Refer to Figure 4-3)
- Click on "Event Bus" button. User navigates to the next screen, data will be transferred from first screen to next screen (Refer to Figure-4.3).

The above described navigation scenario is shown in Figure 4-3

Tutorial 2: Post custom events using Green Robot event bus

The following tutorial will help you to understand how to implement Green Robot event bus to handle the custom events. The steps required to implement the above-specified business scenario are listed below.

1. Work on your configurations
2. Create a main screen layout file.
3. Create navigation screen layout file.
4. Create main activity class
5. Create navigation activity class
6. Create POJO classes
7. Test the application.

The above-specified steps are described in the following sections:

Step 1: Work on your configurations

The following configurations are required to make the Green Robot to work. Add all dependencies to "build.gradle" file. The required dependencies are provided below.

```
compile 'de.greenrobot:eventbus:2.4.0'
```

Step 2: Create a main screen layout file.

Go to res → layout → create "activity_main.xml" file. The following "activity_main.xml" file is used to create the main screen.

```
<RelativeLayout xmlns:android =
    "http://schemas.android.com/apk/res/android"
    xmlns:tools="http://schemas.android.com/tools"
    android:layout_width="match_parent"
    android:layout_height="match_parent"
    android:paddingLeft="@dimen/activity_horizontal_margin"
    android:paddingRight="@dimen/activity_horizontal_margin"
    android:paddingTop="@dimen/activity_vertical_margin"
    android:paddingBottom="@dimen/activity_vertical_margin"
    tools:context=".MainActivity">

    <LinearLayout
        android:layout_width="match_parent"
        android:layout_height="wrap_content"
        android:layout_gravity="center_horizontal"
        android:orientation="vertical">
```

```xml
<TextView
    android:text="First Name"
    android:layout_marginTop="5dp"
    android:enabled="true"
    android:layout_width="match_parent"
    android:layout_height="wrap_content"/>

<EditText
    android:id="@+id/firstName1"
    android:textSize="30sp"
    android:layout_marginTop="5dp"
    android:enabled="true"
    android:layout_width="match_parent"
    android:layout_height="wrap_content"/>

<TextView
    android:text="Last Name"
    android:layout_marginTop="5dp"
    android:enabled="true"
    android:layout_width="match_parent"
    android:layout_height="wrap_content"/>

<EditText
    android:id="@+id/lastName1"
    android:textSize="30sp"
    android:layout_marginTop="5dp"
    android:enabled="true"
    android:layout_width="match_parent"
    android:layout_height="wrap_content"/>

<TextView
    android:text="Age"
    android:layout_marginTop="5dp"
    android:enabled="true"
    android:layout_width="match_parent"
    android:layout_height="wrap_content"/>

<EditText
    android:id="@+id/age1"
    android:textSize="30sp"
    android:layout_marginTop="5dp"
    android:enabled="true"
    android:layout_width="match_parent"
    android:layout_height="wrap_content"/>

<Button
    android:id="@+id/eventbus_button"
    android:layout_width="250dp"
    android:layout_height="wrap_content"
    android:layout_marginBottom="5sp"
    android:layout_marginLeft="60dp"
    android:layout_marginRight="12dp"
    android:enabled="true"
    android:text="Event Bus"
    android:textSize="30sp"/>

</LinearLayout>
```

```
</RelativeLayout>
```

Step 3: Create event bus layout file.

Go to res → layout → create "activity_eventbus.xml" file. The following "activity_eventbus.xml" file is used to create the navigation screen. This layout displays the user specific attributes such as first name, last name, age, and so forth.

```xml
<?xml version="1.0" encoding="utf-8"?>
<LinearLayout xmlns:android="http://schemas.android.com/apk/res/android"
    android:layout_width="fill_parent"
    android:layout_height="fill_parent"
    android:orientation="vertical">

    <TextView
        android:text="First Name"
        android:layout_marginTop="5dp"
        android:enabled="true"
        android:layout_width="match_parent"
        android:layout_height="wrap_content"/>

    <EditText
        android:id="@+id/firstName"
        android:textSize="30sp"
        android:layout_marginTop="5dp"
        android:enabled="true"
        android:layout_width="match_parent"
        android:layout_height="wrap_content"/>

    <TextView
        android:text="Last Name"
        android:layout_marginTop="5dp"
        android:enabled="true"
        android:layout_width="match_parent"
        android:layout_height="wrap_content"/>

    <EditText
        android:id="@+id/lastName"
        android:textSize="30sp"
        android:layout_marginTop="5dp"
        android:enabled="true"
        android:layout_width="match_parent"
        android:layout_height="wrap_content"/>

    <TextView
        android:text="Age"
        android:layout_marginTop="5dp"
        android:enabled="true"
        android:layout_width="match_parent"
        android:layout_height="wrap_content"/>

    <EditText
        android:id="@+id/age"
        android:textSize="30sp"
        android:layout_marginTop="5dp"
        android:enabled="true"
```

```
                    android:layout_width="match_parent"
                    android:layout_height="wrap_content"/>

</LinearLayout>
```

Step 4: Create the main activity classes.

The following `MainActivity.java` class is used to create the main screen with "Event Bus" button. It renders the previously created layout "activity_main.xml" file.

Listing 4-4 provides the main activity class. Note the code inline comments.

Listing 4-4: MainActivity.java class.

```java
package com.example.androidlearning;

import android.app.Activity;
import android.content.Intent;
import android.support.v7.app.ActionBarActivity;
import android.os.Bundle;
import android.view.Menu;
import android.view.MenuItem;
import android.view.View;
import android.widget.Button;
import android.widget.EditText;
import android.widget.TextView;

import com.example.androidlearning.eventbus.EventBusActivity;
import com.example.androidlearning.eventbus.UserDataEvent;

import de.greenrobot.event.EventBus;

// MainActivity.java
public class MainActivity extends Activity {

    @Override
    protected void onCreate(Bundle savedInstanceState) {
        super.onCreate(savedInstanceState);
        setContentView(R.layout.activity_main);

        Button eventBusButton = (Button)
                findViewById(R.id.eventbus_button);
        eventBusButton.setEnabled(true);
        eventBusButton.setOnClickListener(eventBusButtonListener);
    }

    private View.OnClickListener eventBusButtonListener = new
    View.OnClickListener() {
            public void onClick(View v) {
            EditText firstName=(EditText)findViewById(R.id.firstName1);
            EditText lastName =(EditText) findViewById(R.id.lastName1);
            EditText age = (EditText) findViewById(R.id.age1);

            UserDataEvent dataEvent = new UserDataEvent();
            dataEvent.setFirstName(firstName.getText().toString());
            dataEvent.setLastName(lastName.getText().toString());
            dataEvent.setAge(age.getText().toString());
```

```
                    EventBus.getDefault().post(dataEvent);
        }
    };

    /* Called when the EventBus's EventBus.getDefault().
       post(new UserDataEvent()) is invoked. */
    public void onEvent(UserDataEvent userDataEvent) {
        Intent intent = new Intent(this, EventBusActivity.class);
        intent.putExtra("firstName", userDataEvent.getFirstName());
        intent.putExtra("lastName", userDataEvent.getLastName());
        intent.putExtra("age", userDataEvent.getAge());

        startActivity(intent);
    }

    @Override
    // Registering the event bus
    public void onStart() {
        EventBus.getDefault().register(this);
        super.onStart();
    }

    @Override
    // Unregistering the event bus
    public void onStop() {
        EventBus.getDefault().unregister(this);
        super.onStop();
    }
}
```

Step 5: Create the navigation activity classes.

The following `EventBusActivity.java` class is used to create the navigation screen. This class renders the previously created layout "activity_eventbus.xml" file.

Listing 4-5 provides the event bus activity class. Note the code inline comments.

Listing 4-5: EventBusActivity.java class.

```
package com.example.androidlearning.eventbus;

import android.app.Activity;
import android.os.Bundle;
import android.widget.EditText;
import com.example.androidlearning.R;

// EventBusActivity.java
public class EventBusActivity extends Activity {
    @Override
    protected void onCreate(Bundle savedInstanceState) {
        super.onCreate(savedInstanceState);
        setContentView(R.layout.activity_eventbus);
        String firstName = getIntent().getStringExtra("firstName");
        String lastName = getIntent().getStringExtra("lastName");
        String age = getIntent().getStringExtra("age");
```

```
        ((EditText) findViewById(R.id.firstName)).setText(firstName);
        ((EditText) findViewById(R.id.lastName)).setText(lastName);
        ((EditText) findViewById(R.id.age)).setText(age);
    }
}
```

Step 6: Create POJO classes.

The following POJO class is used to store the user-specific details such as first name, last name, and so forth.

```
package com.example.androidlearning.eventbus;

public class UserDataEvent {

    private String firstName;
    private String lastName;
    private String age;

    // Add getter and setter methods
}
```

Step 7: Test the application.

Follow the below provided step-by-step instructions to test the application.

1. Start the emulator
2. Click on application Icon → Main screen will be shown with "Event Bus" button.
3. Click on "Event Bus" button
4. User can view the navigation screen with data (Refer to Figure 4-3)

Advantages

- Provides loosely coupled communication between sender and receiver.
- Works well with Activities, Fragments, and threads
- Simplified communication between sender and receivers
- Provides simple API to handle custom events.

When to use?

- Want to communicate data between two fragments or activities.
- Want to implement publish-subscribe event model in your application.
- Want to handle custom events.

Fragment to Fragment Communication using Event Bus

This tutorial will help you to understand the communication between two fragments using Event bus.

The following business scenario is implemented using Green Robot event bus.

Use Case Scenario:

- Design a main screen with "Fragment" button (Refer to Figure 4-4)
- Click on "Event Bus" button. User navigates to the next screen which contains two fragments. Left side fragment with three buttons, right side fragment shows data (Refer to Figure 4-4).
- Implement fragment to fragment communication using Event bus.

The above described navigation scenario is shown in Figure 4-4.

Figure 4-4: Main and navigation screens

Tutorial 3: Fragment Communication using Event Bus

How to communicate between two fragments using Green robot event bus is illustrated in this tutorial.

1. Create a main screen layout file.
2. Create an activity layout file
3. Create an fragment layout files
4. Create main activity class
5. Create fragments classes
6. Work on your configurations
7. Create POJO classes
8. Test the application.

The above-specified steps are described in the following sections:

Step 1: Create a main screen layout file.

Go to res → layout → update "activity_main.xml" file

Here, reuse the previously created "activity_main.xml" layout file. Add the following button element to the main layout. This layout creates the main screen with Fragment button as shown in Figure 4-4.

```xml
<Button
    android:id="@+id/fragment_button"
    android:layout_marginBottom="5sp"
    android:text="Fragment"
    android:enabled="true"
    android:textSize="30sp"
    android:layout_width="match_parent"
    android:layout_height="wrap_content"
    android:onClick="CallFragment"/>
```

Step 2: Create an activity layout file

Go to res → layout → create "activity_fragment.xml" layout file. This file contains master and detail fragments.

```xml
<?xml version="1.0" encoding="utf-8"?>
<LinearLayout
    xmlns:android="http://schemas.android.com/apk/res/android"
    android:layout_width="fill_parent"
    android:layout_height="fill_parent"
    android:orientation="horizontal" >

    <!-- Fargment 1: Master fragment -->
    <fragment
        android:id="@+id/master_Fragment"
        android:layout_width="0dp"
        android:layout_height="match_parent"
        android:layout_weight="1"
        android:name="com.example.androidlearning.
                        eventbus.MasterFragment"/>

    <!-- Fargment 2: Detail fragment -->
    <fragment
        android:id="@+id/detail_Fragment"
        android:layout_width="0dp"
        android:layout_height="match_parent"
        android:layout_weight="2"
        android:name="com.example.androidlearning.
                        eventbus.DetailFragment"/>

</LinearLayout>
```

Step 3: Create the fragment layout files

Here, create master and detail fragment layout files.

Go to res → layout → create "master_fragment.xml" layout file. This master fragment contains three buttons. The complete layout XML file is provided below.

```xml
<?xml version="1.0" encoding="utf-8"?>
```

```
<LinearLayout
    xmlns:android="http://schemas.android.com/apk/res/android"
    android:layout_width="match_parent"
    android:layout_height="match_parent"
    android:background="#CCFF99"
    android:orientation="vertical"
    android:padding="5dp" >

    <!-- Button 1 -->
    <Button
        android:id="@+id/android_btn_id"
        android:layout_width="wrap_content"
        android:layout_height="wrap_content"
        android:text="Android" />

    <!-- Button 2 -->
    <Button
        android:id="@+id/ios_btn_id"
        android:layout_width="wrap_content"
        android:layout_height="wrap_content"
        android:text="IOS" />

    <!-- Button 3 -->
    <Button
        android:id="@+id/windows_btn_id"
        android:layout_width="wrap_content"
        android:layout_height="wrap_content"
        android:text="Windows" />

</LinearLayout>
```

Go to res → layout → create "details_fragment.xml" layout file. This details fragment contains one text field. The complete layout XML file is provided below.

```
<?xml version="1.0" encoding="utf-8"?>
<LinearLayout xmlns:android="http://schemas.android.com/apk/res/android"
    android:layout_width="match_parent"
    android:layout_height="match_parent"
    android:background="#FFFF99"
    android:orientation="vertical"
    android:padding="20dp" >

    <TextView
        android:id="@+id/display_tv"
        android:layout_width="wrap_content"
        android:layout_height="wrap_content"
        android:text=""
        android:textSize="40sp" />

</LinearLayout>
```

Step 4: Update main activity class

Here, reuse the previously created main activity (MainActivity.java) class. Add the following method to the MainActivity class. The complete method code is provided below. This method receives the button click event and invokes the ActivityFragmet class.

```
public void CallFragment(View view) {
    Intent intent = new Intent(this, ActivityFargment.class);
    startActivity(intent);
}
```

Step 5: Create an activity fragment class

The following `ActivityFragment` class renders the previously created "activity_fragment.xml" file. The complete class code is provided below.

```
package com.example.androidlearning.eventbus;

import android.app.Activity;
import android.os.Bundle;
import com.example.androidlearning.R;

// ActivityFargment.java
public class ActivityFargment extends Activity {

    @Override
    protected void onCreate(Bundle savedInstanceState) {
        super.onCreate(savedInstanceState);
        setContentView(R.layout.activity_fragment);
    }
}
```

Step 5: Create fragments classes

The following `MasterFragment` class inflates the previously created "master_fragment.xml" file. The complete class code is provided below. Note the code inline comments.

```
package com.example.androidlearning.eventbus;

import android.app.Fragment;
import android.os.Bundle;
import android.view.LayoutInflater;
import android.view.View;
import android.view.ViewGroup;
import android.widget.Button;

import com.example.androidlearning.R;
import de.greenrobot.event.EventBus;

// MasterFragment.java
public class MasterFragment extends Fragment {

    @Override
    public View onCreateView(LayoutInflater inflater,
            ViewGroup container,
            Bundle savedInstanceState) {
        View view = inflater.inflate(R.layout.master_fragment,
                container, false);

        // Button instances
        Button android_btn = (Button)
                    view.findViewById(R.id.android_btn_id);
```

```
        Button ios_btn = (Button) view.findViewById(R.id.ios_btn_id);
        Button windows_btn = (Button)
                    view.findViewById(R.id.windows_btn_id);

        // Listener for buttons
        android_btn.setOnClickListener(fargmentButtonListener1);
        ios_btn.setOnClickListener(fargmentButtonListener2);
        windows_btn.setOnClickListener(fargmentButtonListener3);

        return view;
    }

    // Handles the Android button click event
    private View.OnClickListener fargmentButtonListener1 = new
    View.OnClickListener() {
        public void onClick(View v) {
            // Post a message
            EventBus.getDefault().post(new
                    FragmentDataEvent("Android"));
        }
    };

    // Handles the IOS button click event
    private View.OnClickListener fargmentButtonListener2 = new
    View.OnClickListener() {
        public void onClick(View v) {
            // Post a message
            EventBus.getDefault().post(new FragmentDataEvent("IOS"));
        }
    };

    // Handles the Windows button click event
    private View.OnClickListener fargmentButtonListener3 = new
    View.OnClickListener() {
        public void onClick(View v) {
            // Post a message
            EventBus.getDefault().post(new
                    FragmentDataEvent("Windows"));
        }
    };
}
```

Similarly, the following `DetailFragment` class inflates the previously created "detail_fragment.xml" file.

The `onEvent(...)` method of `DetailFragment` class will be invoked automatically, whenever user sends `FragmentDataEvent` event type. The complete class code is provided below. Note the code inline comments.

```
package com.example.androidlearning.eventbus;

import android.app.Fragment;
import android.os.Bundle;
import android.view.LayoutInflater;
import android.view.View;
import android.view.ViewGroup;
```

```java
import android.widget.TextView;

import com.example.androidlearning.R;

import de.greenrobot.event.EventBus;

// DetailFragment.java
public class DetailFragment extends Fragment {

    @Override
    public View onCreateView(LayoutInflater inflater,
            ViewGroup container,
            Bundle savedInstanceState) {
        View view = inflater.inflate(R.layout.details_fragment,
                container, false);
        return view;
    }

    // Event callback method
    public void onEvent(FragmentDataEvent fragmentDataEvent) {
        TextView view = (TextView)
            getView().findViewById(R.id.display_tv);
        view.setText(fragmentDataEvent.getValue());
    }

    @Override
    public void onStart() {
        // Starting event bus
        EventBus.getDefault().register(this);
        super.onStart();
    }

    @Override
    public void onStop() {
        // Stopping event bus
        EventBus.getDefault().unregister(this);
        super.onStop();
    }
}
```

Step 6: Work on your configurations

The following configurations are required to make Green Robot to work. The required dependencies are provided below.

```
compile 'de.greenrobot:eventbus:2.4.0'
```

Add `ActivityFargment` class to the application manifest file. An example code is provided below.

```xml
<activity android:name=".eventbus.ActivityFargment"/>
```

Step 7: Create POJO classes

The following POJO class is used to hold the event data.

```
package com.example.androidlearning.eventbus;

public class FragmentDataEvent {
    private String value;

    public FragmentDataEvent(String value) {
        this.value = value;
    }

    // Add getter and setter methods
}
```

Step 8: Test the application.

Follow the below provided step-by-step instructions to test the application.

1. Start the emulator
2. Click on application Icon → Main screen will be shown with "Fragment" button.
3. Click on "Fragment" button
4. User can view the navigation screen with three buttons (Refer to Figure 4-4)
5. Click on each button to view the data on details fragment.

Dagger

The following business scenario is implemented using Dagger dependency injection framework.

Use Case Scenario:

*   Design a main screen with "Dagger" button (Refer to Figure 4-5)
*   Click on "Dagger" button. User navigates to the next screen (Refer to Figure 4-5).
*   Create and inject the objects using Dagger dependency injection framework.

The above described navigation scenario is shown in Figure 4-5.

Figure 4-5: Main and navigation screens

Tutorial 4: Dependency Injection using Dagger

The following tutorial will help you to understand the use of dependency injection in Android application development. The steps required to implement the above-specified business scenario are listed below.

1. Work on your configurations
2. Create a main screen layout file.
3. Create navigation screen layout file.
4. Create main activity class
5. Create navigation activity class
6. Create POJO classes
7. Test the application.

The above-specified steps are described in the following sections:

Step 1: Work on your configurations

The following configurations are required for Dagger. Add the following dependencies to "build.gradle" file.

```
compile 'com.google.dagger:dagger:2.0'
compile 'javax.inject:javax.inject:1'
apt 'com.google.dagger:dagger-compiler:2.0'
provided 'org.glassfish:javax.annotation:10.0-b28'
```

Add the following plug-in to the "build.gradle" file.

```
apply plugin: 'com.neenbedankt.android-apt'
```

Step 2: Create a main screen layout file.

Go to res → layout → create "activity_main.xml" layout file. The following "activity_main.xml" file is used to create the main screen.

```xml
<RelativeLayout xmlns:android =
    "http://schemas.android.com/apk/res/android"
    xmlns:tools="http://schemas.android.com/tools"
    android:layout_width="match_parent"
    android:layout_height="match_parent"
    android:paddingLeft="@dimen/activity_horizontal_margin"
    android:paddingRight="@dimen/activity_horizontal_margin"
    android:paddingTop="@dimen/activity_vertical_margin"
    android:paddingBottom="@dimen/activity_vertical_margin"
    tools:context=".MainActivity">

    <LinearLayout
        android:layout_width="match_parent"
        android:layout_height="wrap_content"
        android:layout_gravity="center_horizontal"
        android:orientation="vertical">

        <Button
            android:id="@+id/di_button"
            android:layout_width="250dp"
            android:layout_height="wrap_content"
            android:layout_marginBottom="5sp"
            android:layout_marginLeft="60dp"
            android:layout_marginRight="12dp"
            android:enabled="true"
            android:text="Dagger"
            android:textSize="30sp"/>

    </LinearLayout>
</RelativeLayout>
```

Step 3: Create a dagger activity layout file.

Go to res → layout → create "activity_dagger.xml" layout file. The following "activity_dagger.xml" file is used to create the navigation screen.

```xml
<?xml version="1.0" encoding="utf-8"?>
<LinearLayout xmlns:android="http://schemas.android.com/apk/res/android"
    android:layout_width="fill_parent"
    android:layout_height="fill_parent"
    android:orientation="vertical">

    <TextView
        android:text="Speed"
        android:layout_marginTop="5dp"
        android:enabled="true"
        android:layout_width="match_parent"
        android:layout_height="wrap_content"/>

    <EditText
        android:id="@+id/dagger_speed"
```

```
                    android:textSize="30sp"
                    android:layout_marginTop="5dp"
                    android:enabled="true"
                    android:layout_width="match_parent"
                    android:layout_height="wrap_content"/>

</LinearLayout>
```

Step 4: Create the main activity classes.

The following MainActivity.java class is used to create the main screen with "Dagger" button. It renders the previously created "activity_main.xml" file.

Listing 4-6 provides the main activity class. Note the code inline comments.

Listing 4-6: MainActivity.java class.

```java
package com.example.androidlearning;

import android.app.Activity;
import android.content.Intent;
import android.os.Bundle;
import android.view.View;
import android.widget.Button;

import com.example.androidlearning.dagger.DaggerActivity;

// MainActivity.java
public class MainActivity extends Activity {

    @Override
    protected void onCreate(Bundle savedInstanceState) {
        super.onCreate(savedInstanceState);
        setContentView(R.layout.activity_main);

        Button daggerButton = (Button) findViewById(R.id.di_button);
        daggerButton.setEnabled(true);
        daggerButton.setOnClickListener(daggerButtonListener);
    }

    //Create an anonymous class to act as a button click listener
    private View.OnClickListener daggerButtonListener = new
    View.OnClickListener() {
        public void onClick(View v) {
            callDaggerActivity();
        }
    };

    private void callDaggerActivity() {
        Intent intent = new Intent(this, DaggerActivity.class);
        startActivity(intent);
    }
}
```

Step 5: Create navigation activity class

The following `DaggerActivity.java` class is used to create the navigation screen. It renders the previously created "activity_dagger.xml" file.

Listing 4-7 provides the dagger activity class. Note the code inline comments.

Listing 4-7: DaggerActivity.java class.

```
package com.example.androidlearning.dagger;

import android.app.Activity;
import android.os.Bundle;
import android.widget.EditText;
import android.widget.Toast;

import com.example.androidlearning.R;

// DaggerActivity.java
public class DaggerActivity extends Activity {

    @Override
    protected void onCreate(Bundle savedInstanceState) {
        super.onCreate(savedInstanceState);
        setContentView(R.layout.activity_dagger);

        VehicleComponent component = DaggerVehicleComponent.builder().
                    vehicleModule(new VehicleModule()).build();

        Vehicle vehicle = component.provideVehicle();
        vehicle.increaseSpeed(400);

        EditText editText = (EditText) findViewById(R.id.dagger_speed);
        editText.setText(vehicle.getSpeed()+"");
        editText.setBackgroundColor(125);
    }
}
```

Step 6: Create POJO classes

The following POJO classes are used to implement dependency injection. The following `VehicleModule` encapsulates the instances of `Motor` and `Vehicle`.

```
package com.example.androidlearning.dagger;

import javax.inject.Singleton;

import dagger.Module;
import dagger.Provides;

@Module
public class VehicleModule {

    @Provides
    @Singleton
    Motor provideMotor(){
        return new Motor();
    }
```

```
@Provides
@Singleton
Vehicle provideVehicle(){
    return new Vehicle(new Motor());
}
}
```

The `Motor` object code is provided below.

```
package com.example.androidlearning.dagger;

public class Motor {

    private int rpm;

    public int getRpm(){
        return rpm;
    }

    public void increaseSpeed(int value){
        rpm = rpm + value;
    }
}
```

The `Motor` object is injected into the `Vehicle` class. The `Vehicle` object code is provided below.

```
package com.example.androidlearning.dagger;

import javax.inject.Inject;

public class Vehicle {

    private Motor motor;

    @Inject
    public Vehicle(Motor motor){
        this.motor = motor;
    }

    public void increaseSpeed(int value){
        motor.increaseSpeed(value);
    }

    public int getSpeed(){
        return motor.getRpm();
    }
}
```

The `VehicleComponent` interface code is provided below. This is the primary interface used for integrating with `VehicleModule` class.

```
package com.example.androidlearning.dagger;

import javax.inject.Singleton;
```

```
import dagger.Component;

@Singleton
@Component(modules = {VehicleModule.class})
public interface VehicleComponent {
    Vehicle provideVehicle();
}
```

Step 7: Test the application.

Follow the below provided step-by-step instructions to test the application.

1. Start the emulator
2. Click on application Icon → Main screen will be shown with "Dagger" button.
3. Click on "Dagger" button
4. User can view the navigation screen with data (Refer to Figure 4-5)

Advantages

- Avoids unnecessary dependencies
- More reusable code
- Better readability and maintainability
- More testable code

Limitations

- Does not provide the full capabilities like spring dependency injection and IOC container.

When to use?

Dagger is a dependency injection framework for Android. It will create instances of Objects and inject them on dependent classes for use.

Picasso

Tutorial 5: Load and resize the images using Picasso

The following business scenario is implemented using Picasso.

Use Case Scenario:

- Design a main screen with "Picasso" button.
- Click on "Picasso" button. User navigates to the next screen, which shows images of different sizes.

The above described navigation scenario is shown in Figure 4-6.

Figure 4-6: Main and navigation screens

The steps required to implement the above-specified business scenario in Android using Picasso are listed below:

1. Work on your configurations
2. Create a main layout file.
3. Create Picasso layout file.
4. Create Activity classes
5. Test the application.

The above-specified steps are described in the following sections:

Step 1: Work on your configurations

The following configurations are required for Picasso. Add the following dependencies to "build.gradle" file.

```
compile 'com.squareup.picasso:picasso:2.5.2'
```

Step 2: Create a main layout file.

Go to res → layout → create "activity_main.xml" file. The following "activity_main.xml" file is used to create the main screen.

```
<RelativeLayout xmlns:android =
    "http://schemas.android.com/apk/res/android"
    xmlns:tools="http://schemas.android.com/tools"
    android:layout_width="match_parent"
    android:layout_height="match_parent"
    android:paddingLeft="@dimen/activity_horizontal_margin"
    android:paddingRight="@dimen/activity_horizontal_margin"
    android:paddingTop="@dimen/activity_vertical_margin"
```

```
            android:paddingBottom="@dimen/activity_vertical_margin"
            tools:context=".MainActivity">

            <LinearLayout
                android:layout_width="match_parent"
                android:layout_height="wrap_content"
                android:layout_gravity="center_horizontal"
                android:orientation="vertical">

                <Button
                    android:id="@+id/picasso_button"
                    android:layout_width="250dp"
                    android:layout_height="wrap_content"
                    android:layout_marginBottom="5sp"
                    android:layout_marginLeft="60dp"
                    android:layout_marginRight="12dp"
                    android:enabled="true"
                    android:text="Picasso"
                    android:textSize="30sp"/>

            </LinearLayout>
</RelativeLayout>
```

Step 3: Create Picasso layout file.

Go to res → layout → create "activity_picasso.xml" file. The following "activity_picasso.xml" file is used to create the navigation screen.

```
<?xml version="1.0" encoding="utf-8"?>
<LinearLayout xmlns:android="http://schemas.android.com/apk/res/android"
        android:layout_width="fill_parent"
        android:layout_height="fill_parent">

    <ScrollView
        android:layout_width="fill_parent"
        android:layout_height="wrap_content">

        <LinearLayout
            android:layout_width="match_parent"
            android:layout_height="match_parent"
            android:background="#CCFF99"
            android:orientation="vertical"
            android:padding="5dp">

        <ImageView
            android:id="@+id/imageView1"
            android:layout_width="wrap_content"
            android:layout_height="wrap_content"
            android:layout_alignParentTop="true"
            android:layout_centerHorizontal="true"/>

        <ImageView
            android:id="@+id/imageView2"
            android:layout_width="wrap_content"
            android:layout_height="wrap_content"
            android:layout_alignParentTop="true"
```

```
                    android:layout_centerHorizontal="true" />

            <ImageView
                android:id="@+id/imageView3"
                android:layout_width="wrap_content"
                android:layout_height="wrap_content"
                android:layout_alignParentTop="true"
                android:layout_centerHorizontal="true" />

            <ImageView
                android:id="@+id/imageView4"
                android:layout_width="wrap_content"
                android:layout_height="wrap_content"
                android:layout_alignParentTop="true"
                android:layout_centerHorizontal="true" />

        </LinearLayout>
    </ScrollView>
</LinearLayout>
```

Step 4: Create main activity class

The following `MainActivity.java` class is used to create the main screen with "Dagger" button. It renders the previously created "activity_main.xml" file.

Listing 4-8 provides the main activity class. Note the code inline comments.

Listing 4-8: MainActivity.java class.

```java
package com.example.androidlearning;

import android.app.Activity;
import android.content.Intent;
import android.os.Bundle;
import android.view.View;
import android.widget.Button;

import com.example.androidlearning.picasso.PicassoActivity;

// MainActivity.java
public class MainActivity extends Activity {

    @Override
    protected void onCreate(Bundle savedInstanceState) {
        super.onCreate(savedInstanceState);
        setContentView(R.layout.activity_main);

        Button picassoButton=(Button)findViewById(R.id.picasso_button);
        picassoButton.setEnabled(true);
        picassoButton.setOnClickListener(picassoButtonListener);
    }

    // Create an anonymous class to act as a button click listener
    private View.OnClickListener picassoButtonListener = new
    View.OnClickListener() {
        public void onClick(View v) {
            callPicassoActivity();
```

```
        }
    };

    private void callPicassoActivity() {
        Intent intent = new Intent(this, PicassoActivity.class);
        startActivity(intent);
    }
}
```

Step 5: Create navigation activity class

The following `PicassoActivity.java` class is used to create the navigation screen. It renders the previously created "activity_picasso.xml" file.

Listing 4-9 provides the Picasso activity class. Note the code inline comments.

Listing 4-9: PicassoActivity.java class.

```
package com.example.androidlearning.picasso;

import android.app.Activity;
import android.os.Bundle;
import android.widget.ImageView;

import com.example.androidlearning.R;
import com.squareup.picasso.Picasso;

// PicassoActivity.java
public class PicassoActivity extends Activity {

    @Override
    protected void onCreate(Bundle savedInstanceState) {
        super.onCreate(savedInstanceState);
        setContentView(R.layout.activity_picasso);

        ImageView imageView1 =(ImageView)findViewById(R.id.imageView1);
        ImageView imageView2 =(ImageView)findViewById(R.id.imageView2);
        ImageView imageView3 =(ImageView)findViewById(R.id.imageView3);
        ImageView imageView4 =(ImageView)findViewById(R.id.imageView4);

        // Image view
        Picasso.with(this).load(R.drawable.apple).into(imageView1);

        Picasso.with(this).load(R.drawable.apple)
                    .resize(250, 200)
                    .rotate(90)
                    .into(imageView2);

        Picasso.with(this).load(R.drawable.apple)
                .resize(350, 350)
                .rotate(180)
                .into(imageView3);

        Picasso.with(this).load(R.drawable.apple)
                .resize(400, 400)
                .rotate(270)
                .into(imageView4);
```

```
        }
    }
```

Step 6: Test the application.

Follow the below provided step by step instructions to test the application.

1. Start the emulator
2. Click on application Icon → Main screen will be shown with "Picasso" button.
3. Click on "Picasso" button
4. User can view the navigation screen with images (Refer to Figure 4-6)

Advantages

- Simple, easy to use API. Just one line of code.
- Provides image caching capabilities
- Easy to scale, load, resize, and transform the images.

When to use?

Your application want to load, cache, resize, and transform images with less memory.

Summary

Figure 4-7 Android frameworks

This section summarizes the features provided in various Android frameworks. Figure 4-7 summarizes the most important points described in this chapter.

- Spring Android provides an API for invoking REST-based service endpoints.
- The Spring-provided `RestTemplate` class is used to invoke REST-based Web service endpoints.
- `AsyncTask` class is used to execute tasks in background, and it supports both serial and parallel execution.
- Event Bus provides a simplified messaging model between publisher and subscriber.
- Picasso provides an API for loading, caching, and transforming images.
- Dagger provides a simple light-weight dependency injection framework for Android.
- Simple XML is an open-source XML framework used for processing XML in Android.

Chapter 5. Android Material Design Components

Google has introduced Material Design guidelines for Angular, Polymer, and Android. Material design is a specification and set of guidelines for developing visual, motion, interactive, and animation effects in your application. API level 21 is the minimum required target SDK for material design. The Android v7 support library provides widgets for developing material design applications. The primary objective of material design is provide a uniform look and feel across the devices of different screen sizes.

Google released the following projects for developing material design applications.

- Angular – Angular Material
- Polymer – Polymer paper elements
- Android – Themes, widget support libraries, and animation API

The Android material design widgets are listed below. The v7 support library provides these widgets.

- Material Toolbar
- Material Cards and Recycler Views
- Material Notifications
- Material Drawer
- Material Themes
- Elevation API
- Material Animations

This chapter will discuss the following topics:

- Material design guidelines in Android
- Developing Android applications using material design widgets.
- Using material design widgets such as the material toolbar, material cards and recycler views, material notifications, material drawer, themes, and so forth.
- Developing material notifications for handhelds and wearable devices.
- Android material design widgets and support library.
- Translating and rotating animations in Android

What is Material Design and Why Do We Need It?

Material design is a specification for application development which provides a uniform visual experience across devices of different screen sizes. It provides a consistent look and feel across devices and provides a consistent visual experience across various Android devices such as phones, tablets, Google Glass, Android TV, smart watches, and so forth. With the material design standard, the application developers don't have to write unique code for every device.

Android provides the following components for building material design applications.

- Material themes

- Material widgets
- New API for Animations and shadow views

Material design provides the following benefits.

- Allows a consistent visual experience across devices of different sizes.
- Maintains consistent look and feel across applications
- Allows code reusability and maintainability

Material design widgets provide uniform visual experiences across the devices as shown in Figure 5-1.

Figure 5-1: Material design widgets for various devices

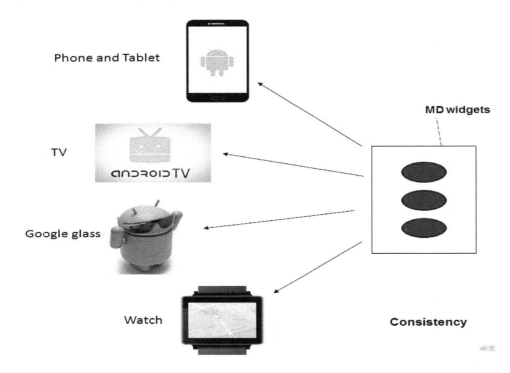

Material Toolbar

The material toolbar is a UI element which can contain icons, images, and menus. The toolbar can be customized with material colors and themes. In general, an Android toolbar can contain the following elements. An example toolbar is shown in Figure 5-2.

- Title and sub title
- Image buttons
- Menus and menu items.

The Android-provided `AppCompatActivity` class can be used to implement the material toolbar in application development. Your activity class must extend the `AppCompatActivity` class. An example class code is provided below.

```
public class ToolbarActivity extends AppCompatActivity {
    ...
}
```

Figure 5-2: Material toolbar with icon, title, and menu

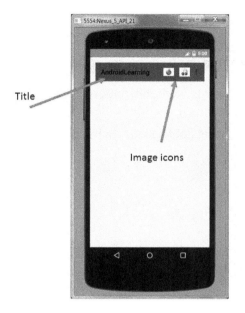
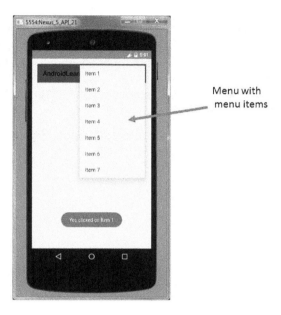

The `ActionBarActivity` class was deprecated. Older versions of the Android still support the `ActionBarActivity` class. An example class code is provided below.

```
public class ToolbarActivity extends ActionBarActivity {
    ...
    // ActionBarActivity class is deprecated.
}
```

An example of the toolbar widget provided with Android's support library is given below.

```
<?xml version="1.0" encoding="utf-8"?>
<android.support.v7.widget.Toolbar
    android:id="@+id/mat_app_toolbar"
    xmlns:android="http://schemas.android.com/apk/res/android">

    ...

</android.support.v7.widget.Toolbar>
```

NOTE: Tutorial -1 provides complete details on implementing the material toolbar

---

Material Notifications

Notifications undergo visual changes consistent with the material design specification. Notifications can be extendable to wearable devices. The new material notifications has the following characteristics.

- Notifications are shown in device lock screen
- Notifications are shown in reverse chronological order
- By default, priority of notifications are based on its timestamp.
- Android now supports heads-up notifications – a new format for high-priority notifications while device is in use.
- Android supports wearable notifications – Can be extended to wearable devices.

A notification can have the following attributes. Figure 5-3 shows notifications on handheld and wearable devices.

- Icon
- Name
- Description
- Time stamp

Figure 5-3: Material notifications with icon, title, description, and time stamp

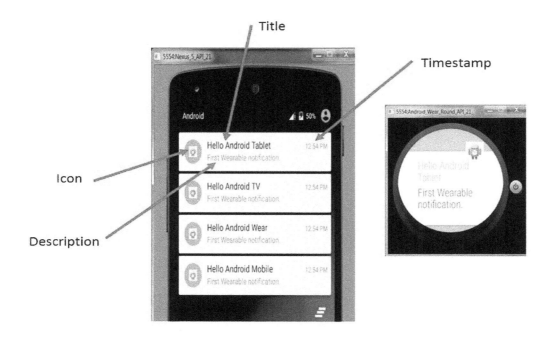

NOTE: Tutorial -3 provides complete details on implementing material notifications.

Material Themes

The material themes are available only in Android 5.0 and API level 21. The v7 support library provides themes with material colors to customize the widgets. You can customize the application with the brand and colors required by your organization. The material themes supports the following styles.

- Dark version - `@android:style/Theme.Material`
- Light version - `@android:style/Theme.Material.Light`
- Light version with dark action bar - `@android:style/Theme.Material.Light.DarkActionbar`

Apply the above material themes in your application manifest file and view the output. The different material themes are shown in Figure 5-4.

Figure 5-4: Material themes

Dark Material Theme   Light Material Theme   Light Material Theme with Dark Action bar

An example use of the above listed material themes is provided below. The material theme listed below displays the dark version.

```
<application
    android:allowBackup="true"
    android:icon="@drawable/ic_launcher"
    android:label="@string/app_name"
    android:theme="@android:style/Theme.Material">
    ...
</application>
```

The material theme listed below displays the light version.

```
<application
    android:allowBackup="true"
    android:icon="@drawable/ic_launcher"
    android:label="@string/app_name"
    android:theme="@android:style/Theme.Material.Light">
    ...
</application>
```

The material theme listed below displays the light version with dark action bar.

```
<application
        android:allowBackup="true"
        android:icon="@drawable/ic_launcher"
        android:label="@string/app_name"
        android:theme=
        "@android:style/Theme.Material.Light.DarkActionBar">
    ...
</application>
```

The following example illustrates the use of material colors for "App bar", "Status bar", and other UI elements. Note the code inline comments.

```
<!-- inherit from the material theme -->
<style name="MyAppTheme" parent="android:Theme.Material">
    <!-- your app branding color for the app bar -->
    <item name="android:colorPrimary">@color/material_grey_800</item>

    <!-- darker variant for the status bar and contextual app bars -->
    <item name="android:colorPrimaryDark">
        @color/primary_dark_material_dark
    </item>

    <!-- theme UI controls like checkboxes and text fields -->
    <item name="android:colorAccent">@color/material_grey_600</item>
</style>
```

Use the "MyAppTheme" created above in your application manifest. An example code is provided below.

```
<application
    android:allowBackup="true"
    android:icon="@drawable/ic_launcher"
    android:label="@string/app_name"
    android:theme="@android:style/MyAppTheme">
    ...
</application>
```

Material Animations

Android 5.0 (API level 21) supports material animations and animated vector drawables (AVD). You can define and implement custom animations in Android applications.

The following code animates an image linearly.

```
ImageView androidImageView = (ImageView) findViewById(R.id.anim_apple);
```

```
TranslateAnimation animation =
            new TranslateAnimation(0.0f, 400.0f, 0.0f, 0.0f);
animation.setDuration(5000);
animation.setRepeatCount(Animation.INFINITE);
animation.setRepeatMode(2);
animation.setFillAfter(true);
androidImageView.startAnimation(animation);
```

The following code animates an image circularly.

```
RotateAnimation anim = new RotateAnimation(0f, 350f, 350f, 700f);
anim.setInterpolator(new LinearInterpolator());
anim.setRepeatCount(Animation.INFINITE);
anim.setDuration(700);
ImageView androidImageView = (ImageView) findViewById(R.id.anim_apple);
androidImageView.setAnimation(anim);
```

The benefits of animated vector drawables are listed below.

- You can define the graphical images into a XML
- User can animate the each and every XML element and attribute of an image.
- The quality of the graphics does not reduce if you enlarge or zoom the image.

The following XML vector defines the head and eyes of a green robot. You can animate each XML element and attribute independently.

```
<?xml version="1.0" encoding="utf-8"?>
<vector xmlns:android="http://schemas.android.com/apk/res/android"
    android:viewportWidth="500"
    android:viewportHeight="500"
    android:width="500px"
    android:height="500px">

    <group android:name="greenrobot">
        <group android:name="head_eyes">
            <path
                android:name="head"
                android:fillColor="#9FBF3B"
                android:pathData="..."/>
            <path
                android:name="left_eye"
                android:fillColor="#FFFFFF"
                android:pathData="..."/>
            <path
                android:name="right_eye"
                android:fillColor="#FFFFFF"
                android:pathData="..." />
        </group>
    </group>
</vector>
```

Material Cards and Recycler Views

A `RecyclerView` widget is a pluggable version of the list view. This widget is used to display the data lists. A `RecyclerView` widget is used to display the collection of data objects. This widget provides a scrollable view. An example use of this widget is provided below.

```
<android.support.v7.widget.RecyclerView
    android:id="@+id/cardList"
    android:layout_width="match_parent"
    android:layout_height="match_parent"/>
```

The `CardView` widget is used to display the pieces of information in cards. Each card contains one row of data; each card represents one row in a recycler view. An example use of this widget is provided below. In this example, each card contains one image and two text fields as shown in Figure 5-5.

```
<android.support.v7.widget.CardView
    xmlns:android="http://schemas.android.com/apk/res/android"
    xmlns:card_view="http://schemas.android.com/apk/res-auto"
    android:id="@+id/card_view"
    android:layout_width="match_parent"
    android:layout_height="match_parent"
    android:layout_margin="5dp"
    android:orientation="horizontal"
    card_view:cardBackgroundColor="@android:color/black"
    card_view:cardCornerRadius="5dp">

    <LinearLayout
        android:layout_width="match_parent"
        android:layout_height="wrap_content"
        android:orientation="vertical">

        <ImageView
            android:id="@+id/vizagbeach"/>

        <TextView
            android:id="@+id/countryName"
            android:textSize="24dp" />

        <TextView
            android:id="@+id/countryDetails"
            android:textSize="24dp" />

    </LinearLayout>
</android.support.v7.widget.CardView>
```

Figure 5-5 shows the cards and the recycler view widget. Each card contains one image and two text fields.

Figure 5-5: Cards and recycler view

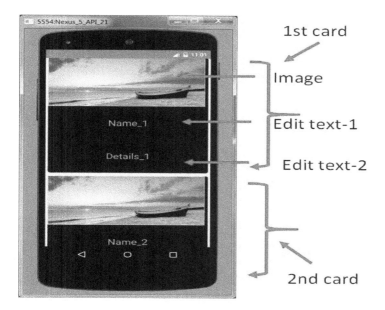

Cards and Recycler View

The following code is used to integrate the recycler view widget with card view widget.

```
RecyclerView recList = (RecyclerView) findViewById(R.id.cardList);
recList.setHasFixedSize(true);

CardsAdapter ca = new CardsAdapter(createList(10), this);
recList.setAdapter(ca);
```

What does the `CardsAdapter` class do?

The Adapter class must extend the `RecyclerView.Adapter` class. This adapter class is an intermediate class between recycler view and the dataset. The adapter class obtains the data from the dataset; and passes it to the UI layout manger to display it on the screen.

This adapter class must override the `onBindViewHolder(...)` and `onCreateViewHolder(...)` methods. The structure of the recycler view adapter class is provided below.

```
public class CardsAdapter extends
        RecyclerView.Adapter<CardsAdapter.CountryViewHolder> {
    ...

    @Override
    public void onBindViewHolder(CountryViewHolder countryViewHolder,
        int i) {
        ...
    }

    @Override
    public CountryViewHolder onCreateViewHolder(ViewGroup viewGroup,
```

```
        int i) {
            ...
    }

    public static class CountryViewHolder extends
            RecyclerView.ViewHolder {
        ...
    }

}
```

NOTE: Tutorial -2 provides the complete details on implementing cards and the recycler view

---

View Shadows

Material design introduces the elevation property for UI elements. In addition to X and Y properties, Android provides a Z property for UI elements. The Z -property represents the elevation view. The `setElevation(...)` method of UI elements can be used to set the elevation. An example use of elevation API is provided below.

```
TextView tv = new TextView(this);
tv.setText("Comments:");
tv.setEnabled(true);
tv.setTextSize(25.00f);
tv.setBackgroundColor(Color.WHITE);
tv.setElevation(75.0f);
```

Similarly, you can use XML attribute provided below to set the elevation in your layout files.

```
<TextView
    android:layout_width="wrap_content"
    android:layout_height="wrap_content"
    android:background="@drawable/rectangle"
    android:text="Hallo World"
    android:padding="8dp"
    android:elevation="75dp"/>
```

Material Navigation Drawer

The material navigation drawer is a most commonly found pattern in Google applications; it slides from left to right with a toggled hamburger icon on the toolbar. A material drawer is used for navigating to various pages in your application. You can build your own material drawer using the material toolbar, cards and recycler views. More details about this topic discussed in Chapter -10.

Material Toolbar

Tutorial 1: Implementing Material Toolbar

The following business scenario is implemented to demonstrate material toolbar.

Use Case Scenario:

- Design a main screen with "ToolBar" button.
- Click on "ToolBar" button. New screen will be displayed with a toolbar and menu (See Figure 5-6)
- Click on toolbar menu icon.
- Menu will be shown with menu items (See Figure 5-6)
- Click on menu item (item 1) → user can view the "You selected Item1" message on screen.

The above described navigation scenario is shown in Figure 5-6.

Figure 5-6: Material toolbar with menu and menu items

  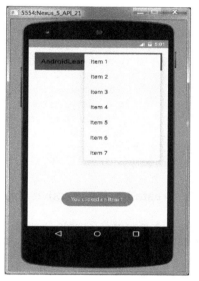

The steps required to implement the above-specified business scenario in Android are listed below:

1. Create a main activity layout file.
2. Create toolbar activity layout file.
3. Create "menu_toolbar.xml" file
4. Update "styles.xml" file
5. Create Activity classes
6. Test the application.

The above-specified steps are described in the following sections:

Step 1: Create a main activity layout file

Go to res → layout → create "activity_main.xml" layout file. The following "activity_main.xml" file is used to create the main screen.

```
<RelativeLayout xmlns:android =
    "http://schemas.android.com/apk/res/android"
    xmlns:tools="http://schemas.android.com/tools"
    android:layout_width="match_parent"
```

```
android:layout_height="match_parent"
android:paddingLeft="@dimen/activity_horizontal_margin"
android:paddingRight="@dimen/activity_horizontal_margin"
android:paddingTop="@dimen/activity_vertical_margin"
android:paddingBottom="@dimen/activity_vertical_margin"
tools:context=".MainActivity">

    <LinearLayout
        android:layout_width="match_parent"
        android:layout_height="wrap_content"
        android:layout_gravity="center_horizontal"
        android:orientation="vertical">

        <Button
            android:id="@+id/toolbar_button"
            android:layout_width="250dp"
            android:layout_height="wrap_content"
            android:layout_marginBottom="5sp"
            android:layout_marginLeft="60dp"
            android:layout_marginRight="12dp"
            android:enabled="true"
            android:text="ToolBar"
            android:textSize="30sp"/>

    </LinearLayout>
</RelativeLayout>
```

Step 2: Create a toolbar activity layout file

Go to res → layout → create "activity_toolbar.xml" layout file. The following "activity_toolbar.xml" file is used to create a screen with toolbar. This layout displays toolbar with menu (Refer to Figure 5-6)

```
<RelativeLayout xmlns:android="http://schemas.android.com/
    apk/res/android"
    xmlns:tools="http://schemas.android.com/tools"
    android:layout_width="match_parent"
    android:layout_height="match_parent"
    android:paddingBottom="@dimen/activity_vertical_margin"
    android:paddingLeft="@dimen/activity_horizontal_margin"
    android:paddingRight="@dimen/activity_horizontal_margin"
    android:paddingTop="@dimen/activity_vertical_margin">

    <LinearLayout
        android:layout_width="match_parent"
        android:layout_height="wrap_content"
        android:layout_gravity="center_horizontal"
        android:orientation="vertical">

        <!-- Including app_bar.xml file -->
        <include android:id="@+id/app_bar" layout="@layout/app_bar"/>

    </LinearLayout>
</RelativeLayout>
```

Include the below provided "app_bar.xml" file into the activity layout "activity_toolbar.xml" file. This file contains the Toolbar widget.

```xml
<?xml version="1.0" encoding="utf-8"?>
<android.support.v7.widget.Toolbar
    android:id="@+id/mat_app_toolbar"
    android:layout_width="match_parent"
    android:layout_height="match_parent"
    android:background="@color/material_blue_grey_800"
    android:elevation="150dp"
    xmlns:android="http://schemas.android.com/apk/res/android">

</android.support.v7.widget.Toolbar>
```

Step 3: Create a "menu_toolbar.xml" file

Go to res → menu → create "menu_toolbar.xml" file.

When you create your android project, android studio creates the "menu_main.xml" file in "menu" directory. Create a new menu file in "menu" directory and the file is named the "menu_toolbar.xml". The following code is used to add image icons to the toolbar.

```xml
<?xml version="1.0" encoding="utf-8"?>
<menu xmlns:android="http://schemas.android.com/apk/res/android"
    xmlns:app="http://schemas.android.com/apk/res-auto"
    android:layout_width="match_parent"
    android:layout_height="wrap_content">;

    <item
        android:id="@+id/new_game"
        android:icon="@drawable/apple"
        android:title="Item 1"
        app:showAsAction="ifRoom"/>

    <item
        android:id="@+id/help"
        android:icon="@drawable/cherry"
        android:title="Item 2"
        app:showAsAction="always"/>

</menu>
```

Step 4: Update "styles.xml" file

Go to res → values → styles → update "styles.xml" file.

When you create your android project, android studio creates "styles.xml" file in "values" directory. Update the application theme in this file. Updated XML file is provided below.

```xml
<resources>
    <!-- Base application theme. Use this for toolbar/appbar -->
    <style name="AppTheme" parent="Theme.AppCompat.Light.NoActionBar">
        <!-- Customize your theme here. -->
    </style>
</resources>
```

Step 5: Create Main Activity class

The following `MainActivity.java` class is used to create the main screen with "ToolBar" button. It renders the previously created "activity_main.xml" file.

Listing 5-1 provides the main activity class. Note the code inline comments.

Listing 5-1: MainActivity.java class.

```
package com.example.androidlearning;

import android.app.Activity;
import android.content.Intent;
import android.os.Bundle;
import android.view.Menu;
import android.view.MenuItem;
import android.view.View;
import android.widget.Button;

import com.example.androidlearning.md.ToolbarActivity;

// MainActivity.java
public class MainActivity extends Activity {

    @Override
    protected void onCreate(Bundle savedInstanceState) {
        super.onCreate(savedInstanceState);
        setContentView(R.layout.activity_main);

        // Button event listener to capture the click event
        Button toolbarButton=(Button)findViewById(R.id.toolbar_button);
        toolbarButton.setEnabled(true);
        toolbarButton.setOnClickListener(toolbarButtonListener);
    }

    // Create an anonymous class to act as a button click listener
    private View.OnClickListener toolbarButtonListener = new
    View.OnClickListener() {
        public void onClick(View v) {
            callToolbarActivity();
        }
    };

    private void callToolbarActivity() {
        Intent intent = new Intent(this, ToolbarActivity.class);
        startActivity(intent);
    }
}
```

Step 6: Create Toolbar Activity class

The following `ToolbarActivity` class is used to create the toolbar with menu. It uses the previously created "activity_toolbar.xml" file.

Listing 5-2 provides the Toolbar activity class. Note the code inline comments.

Listing 5-2: ToolbarActivity.java class.

```java
package com.example.androidlearning.md;

import android.os.Bundle;
import android.support.v7.app.ActionBarActivity;
import android.support.v7.widget.Toolbar;
import android.util.Log;
import android.view.Menu;
import android.view.MenuItem;
import android.widget.Toast;

import com.example.androidlearning.R;

// ToolbarActivity.java
public class ToolbarActivity extends ActionBarActivity {

    private Toolbar toolbar;

    @Override
    protected void onCreate(Bundle savedInstanceState) {
        super.onCreate(savedInstanceState);
        setContentView(R.layout.activity_toolbar);

        toolbar = (Toolbar) findViewById(R.id.app_bar);
        setSupportActionBar(toolbar);
    }

    @Override
    // Creates a Toolbar with menu
    public boolean onCreateOptionsMenu(Menu menu) {
        getMenuInflater().inflate(R.menu.menu_toolbar, menu);
        CreateMenu(menu);

        return true;
    }

    // Adding menu items to the Toolbar menu
    private void CreateMenu(Menu menu_new) {
        MenuItem mnu1 = menu_new.add(0, 0, 0, "Item 1");
        {
            mnu1.setAlphabeticShortcut('a');
            mnu1.setIcon(R.drawable.ic_launcher);
        }

        MenuItem mnu2 = menu_new.add(0, 1, 1, "Item 2");
        {
            mnu2.setAlphabeticShortcut('b');
            mnu2.setIcon(R.drawable.ic_launcher);
        }

        MenuItem mnu3 = menu_new.add(0, 2, 2, "Item 3");
        {
            mnu3.setAlphabeticShortcut('c');
            mnu3.setIcon(R.drawable.ic_launcher);
        }
```

```java
        menu_new.add(0, 3, 3, "Item 4");
        menu_new.add(0, 4, 4, "Item 5");
        menu_new.add(0, 5, 5, "Item 6");
        menu_new.add(0, 6, 6, "Item 7");
    }

    @Override
    // Receives the menu item selected events
    public boolean onOptionsItemSelected(MenuItem item) {
        return MenuChoice(item);
    }

    // Implement your menu item selection event
    private boolean MenuChoice(MenuItem item) {
        switch (item.getItemId()) {
            case 0:
                // Implement your navigation logic here ...
                Toast.makeText(this, "You clicked on Item 1",
                        Toast.LENGTH_LONG).show();
                return true;
            case 1:
                Toast.makeText(this, "You clicked on Item 2",
                        Toast.LENGTH_LONG).show();
                return true;
            case 2:
                Toast.makeText(this, "You clicked on Item 3",
                        Toast.LENGTH_LONG).show();
                return true;
            case 3:
                Toast.makeText(this, "You clicked on Item 4",
                        Toast.LENGTH_LONG).show();
                return true;
            case 4:
                Toast.makeText(this, "You clicked on Item 5",
                        Toast.LENGTH_LONG).show();
                return true;
            case 5:
                Toast.makeText(this, "You clicked on Item 6",
                        Toast.LENGTH_LONG).show();
                return true;
            case 6:
                Toast.makeText(this, "You clicked on Item 7",
                        Toast.LENGTH_LONG).show();
                return true;
        }
        return false;
    }
}
```

Step 7: Test the application

Follow the below provided step-by-step instructions to test the application.

1. Start the emulator
2. Click on application Icon → Main screen will be shown with "Toolbar" button.
3. Click on "Toolbar" button

4. New screen will be displayed with Toolbar and menu (Shown in Figure 5-6)
5. Click on menu icon → Menu items will be shown (Shown in Figure 5-6)
6. Click on "Item 1" → Selected item text will be displayed on the screen.

You can implement the next level navigation logic in menu choice selection event.

Cards and Recycler Views

Tutorial 2: Cards and Recycler Views

The following business scenario is implemented to demonstrate material cards and recycler view widgets.

Use Case Scenario:

- Design a main screen with "Show Cards" button.
- Click on "Show Cards" button. New screen will be shown with image, name, and details card. (See Figure 5-7)
- User can scroll up-and-down to see the cards.

The above described navigation scenario is shown in Figure 5-7.

Figure 5-7: Material cards and recycler view

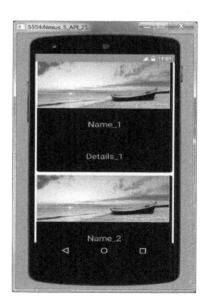

The steps required to implement the above-specified business scenario in Android are listed below:

1. Work on your configurations
2. Create a main activity layout file.
3. Create cards activity layout file.
4. Create recycler view activity layout file

5. Create cards activity class
6. Create cards adapter class
7. Test the application.

The above-specified steps are described in the following sections:

Step 1: Work on your configurations

Add the cards and recycler view dependencies to "build.gradle" file. The required dependencies are provided below.

```
compile 'com.android.support:recyclerview-v7:21.+'
compile 'com.android.support:cardview-v7:21.+'
```

Step 2: Create a main activity layout file

Go to res → layout → create "activity_main.xml" layout file. The following "activity_main.xml" file is used to create the main screen.

```
<RelativeLayout xmlns:android =
     "http://schemas.android.com/apk/res/android"
     xmlns:tools="http://schemas.android.com/tools"
     android:layout_width="match_parent"
     android:layout_height="match_parent"
     android:paddingLeft="@dimen/activity_horizontal_margin"
     android:paddingRight="@dimen/activity_horizontal_margin"
     android:paddingTop="@dimen/activity_vertical_margin"
     android:paddingBottom="@dimen/activity_vertical_margin"
     tools:context=".MainActivity">

     <LinearLayout
          android:layout_width="match_parent"
          android:layout_height="wrap_content"
          android:layout_gravity="center_horizontal"
          android:orientation="vertical">

          <Button
               android:id="@+id/cards_button"
               android:layout_width="250dp"
               android:layout_height="wrap_content"
               android:layout_marginBottom="5sp"
               android:layout_marginLeft="60dp"
               android:layout_marginRight="12dp"
               android:enabled="true"
               android:text="ToolBar"
               android:textSize="30sp"/>

     </LinearLayout>
</RelativeLayout>
```

Step 3: Create cards activity layout file.

Go to res → layout → create "activity_cardsview.xml" file.

The following "activity_cardsview.xml" file is used to create cards layout screen. This layout displays the cards view to the user (Refer to Figure 5-7)

```xml
<?xml version="1.0" encoding="utf-8"?>
<android.support.v7.widget.CardView
    xmlns:android="http://schemas.android.com/apk/res/android"
    xmlns:card_view="http://schemas.android.com/apk/res-auto"
    android:id="@+id/card_view"
    android:layout_width="match_parent"
    android:layout_height="match_parent"
    android:layout_margin="5dp"
    android:orientation="horizontal"
    card_view:cardBackgroundColor="@android:color/black"
    card_view:cardCornerRadius="5dp">

    <LinearLayout
        android:layout_width="match_parent"
        android:layout_height="wrap_content"
        android:orientation="vertical">

        <ImageView
            android:id="@+id/vizagbeach"
            android:layout_width="wrap_content"
            android:layout_height="wrap_content"
            android:src="@drawable/vizagbeach"
            android:contentDescription="@null"/>

        <TextView
            android:id="@+id/countryName"
            android:layout_width="match_parent"
            android:layout_height="100dp"
            android:layout_centerInParent="true"
            android:background="?android:selectableItemBackground"
            android:clickable="true"
            android:focusable="true"
            android:gravity="center"
            android:textColor="@android:color/holo_blue_light"
            android:textSize="24dp" />

        <TextView
            android:id="@+id/countryDetails"
            android:layout_width="match_parent"
            android:layout_height="100dp"
            android:layout_centerInParent="true"
            android:background="?android:selectableItemBackground"
            android:clickable="true"
            android:focusable="true"
            android:gravity="center"
            android:textColor="@android:color/holo_blue_light"
            android:textSize="24dp" />

    </LinearLayout>
</android.support.v7.widget.CardView>
```

Step 4: Create recycler view activity layout file

Go to res → layout → create "activity_recyclerview.xml" file.

The following "activity_recyclerview.xml" file is used to create recycler view layout.

```
<RelativeLayout
    xmlns:android="http://schemas.android.com/apk/res/android"
    xmlns:tools="http://schemas.android.com/tools"
    android:layout_width="match_parent"
    android:layout_height="match_parent">

    <android.support.v7.widget.RecyclerView
        android:id="@+id/cardList"
        android:layout_width="match_parent"
        android:layout_height="match_parent"/>

</RelativeLayout>
```

Step 5: Create cards activity class

The following CardsActivity class is used to create the cards view layout. This class renders the previously created "activity_recyclerview.xml" file.

Listing 5-3 provides the cards activity class. Note the code inline comments.

Listing 5-3: CardsActivity.java class.

```
package com.example.androidlearning.md;

import android.app.Activity;
import android.os.Bundle;
import android.support.v7.widget.LinearLayoutManager;
import android.support.v7.widget.RecyclerView;

import com.example.androidlearning.R;

import java.util.ArrayList;
import java.util.List;

// CardsActivity.java
public class CardsActivity extends Activity {

    @Override
    protected void onCreate(Bundle savedInstanceState) {
        super.onCreate(savedInstanceState);
        setContentView(R.layout.activity_recyclerview);

        RecyclerView recList=(RecyclerView)findViewById(R.id.cardList);
        recList.setHasFixedSize(true);

        LinearLayoutManager llm = new LinearLayoutManager(this);
        llm.setOrientation(LinearLayoutManager.VERTICAL);
        recList.setLayoutManager(llm);

        CardsAdapter ca = new CardsAdapter(createList(10), this);
        recList.setAdapter(ca);
    }
```

```
        private List<CountryData> createList(int size) {
            List<CountryData> result = new ArrayList<CountryData>();
            for (int i = 1; i <= size; i++) {
                CountryData cd = new CountryData();
                cd.setName(CountryData.NAME_PREFIX + i);
                cd.setCountryDetails(CountryData.DETAILS_PREFIX + i);
                result.add(cd);
            }
            return result;
        }
}
```

Step 6: Create cards adapter class

The following `CardsAdapter` class extends the `RecyclerView.Adapter` class. This class renders the previously created "activity_cardview.xml" file.

Listing 5-4 provides the cards adapter class. Note the code inline comments

Listing 5-4: CardsAdapter.java class.

```
package com.example.androidlearning.md;

import android.content.Context;
import android.support.v7.widget.RecyclerView;
import android.view.LayoutInflater;
import android.view.View;
import android.view.ViewGroup;
import android.widget.TextView;

import java.util.List;
import com.example.androidlearning.R;

// CardsAdapter.java
public class CardsAdapter extends
        RecyclerView.Adapter<CardsAdapter.CountryViewHolder> {

    private List<CountryData> countryDataList;
    private Context mContext;

    public CardsAdapter(List<CountryData> countryDataList,
            Context context) {
        this.countryDataList = countryDataList;
        this.mContext = context;
    }

    @Override
    public int getItemCount() {
        return countryDataList.size();
    }

    @Override
    public void onBindViewHolder(CountryViewHolder countryViewHolder,
                        int i) {
        CountryData cd = countryDataList.get(i);
        countryViewHolder.name.setText(cd.getName());
```

```
        countryViewHolder.countryDetails.setText(
                        cd.getCountryDetails());
    }

    @Override
    public CountryViewHolder onCreateViewHolder(ViewGroup viewGroup,
                                        int i) {
        View itemView = LayoutInflater.from(viewGroup.getContext()).
                inflate(R.layout.activity_cardview, viewGroup, false);
        return new CountryViewHolder(itemView);
    }

    public static class CountryViewHolder extends
                                RecyclerView.ViewHolder {
        public TextView name;
        public TextView countryDetails;

        public CountryViewHolder(View v) {
            super(v);
            name = (TextView) v.findViewById(R.id.countryName);
            countryDetails = (TextView)
                    v.findViewById(R.id.countryDetails);
            countryDetails.getText());
        }
    }
}
```

Step 7: Create a model object

```
package com.example.androidlearning.md;

public class CountryData {

    private String name;
    private String countryDetails;

    // Add getter and setters

}
```

Step 8: Test the application

Follow the below provided step-by-step instructions to test the application.

1. Start the emulator
2. Click on application Icon → Main screen will be displayed with "Show Cards" button.
3. Click on "Show Cards" button
4. New screen will be shown with 10 cards – It displays the image, name, and description of each card (Shown in Figure 5-7)
5. User can navigate up-and-down to view the cards.

Material Notifications (Mobile and Wear)

Tutorial 3: Handheld and Wearable Notifications

The following business scenario is implemented to demonstrate material wearable notifications for handheld and wearable.

Use Case Scenario:

- Show notifications on handheld and wearable devices.
- Create four notifications for phone and watch (See Figure 5-8)
- Illustrate the notification implementation details for phone and watch (See Figure 5-8).

The above described business scenario is shown in Figure 5-8.

Figure 5-8: Material notifications for phone and watch

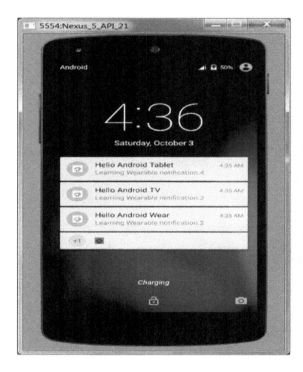

The steps required to implement the above-specified business scenario in Android are listed below:

1. Configure a new project
2. Create handheld activity class
3. Create wearable activity class
4. Run the application in Phone emulator
5. Run the application in Watch emulator

The above-specified steps are described in the following sections:

Step 1: Configure a new project

Create a new Android project for handheld and wearable's. The step by step instructions are provided below.

Create a new project → File → Create new project.

Figure 5-9: Creating a new wearable project

Select Phone and Wear platforms. Select minimum SDK for Phone and Wear modules as shown in Figure 5-10

Figure 5-10: Selecting phone, tablet, and wear

Select blank activity for mobile module.

Figure 5-11: Selecting activity template

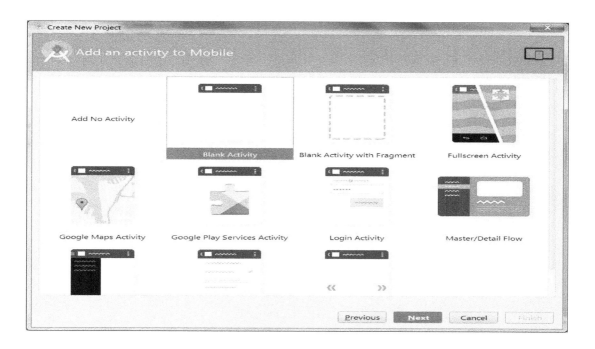

Leave the default vales as shown in Figure 5-12

Figure 5-12: Activity metadata

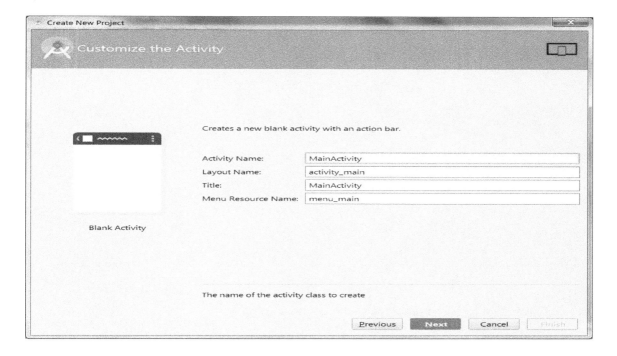

Select the activity for wearable device.

Figure 5-13: Selecting activity for wearable device

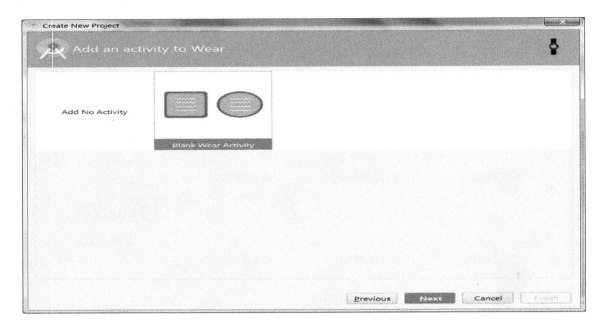

Create a blank activity for the wearable device.

Figure 5-14: Wearable activity metadata

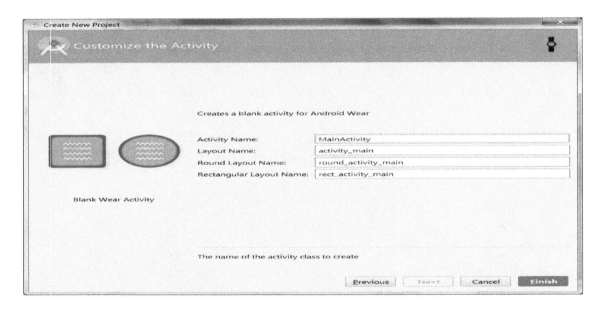

Click on Finish. The following progress dialog will be shown.

Figure 5-15: Progress dialog

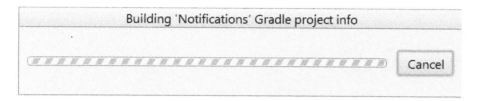

The structure of the newly created project is shown in Figure 5-16. This project contains "mobile" and "wear" modules.

Figure 5-16: Mobile and Wear projects in Android studio explorer

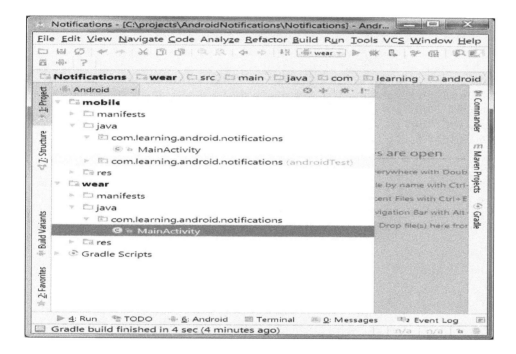

Step 3: Use the default created layout files.

Use the default created "activity_main.xml" files of the mobile and wearable module.

Step 4: Create handheld activity class

The following `MainActivity.java` class is used for "mobile" module. This class renders the default created "activity_main.xml" layout file.

Listing 5-5 provides the main activity class. Note the code inline comments.

Listing 5-5: MainActivity.java class

```
package com.learning.android.notifications;

import android.app.Notification;
import android.support.v4.app.NotificationCompat;
```

```java
import android.support.v4.app.NotificationManagerCompat;
import android.os.Bundle;
import android.support.v7.app.AppCompatActivity;

import java.util.ArrayList;
import java.util.List;

// MainActivity.java
public class MainActivity extends AppCompatActivity {

    @Override
    protected void onCreate(Bundle savedInstanceState) {
        super.onCreate(savedInstanceState);
        setContentView(R.layout.activity_main);

        createNotifications();
    }

    // Method creates wearable notifications
    private void createNotifications() {
        List<String> titles = new ArrayList<String>();
        titles.add("Hello Android Mobile");
        titles.add("Hello Android Wear");
        titles.add("Hello Android TV");
        titles.add("Hello Android Tablet");

        for (int i = 0; i < titles.size(); i++) {
            // Shown in wear
            NotificationCompat.WearableExtender wearableExtender =
                new NotificationCompat.WearableExtender()
                    .setHintShowBackgroundOnly(true);

            // Shown in Handheld
            Notification notification = new
                    NotificationCompat.Builder(this)
                    .setSmallIcon(R.drawable.ic_launcher)
                    .setContentTitle(titles.get(i))
                    .setContentText("Learning Wearable notification."
                    + (i+1)).extend(wearableExtender)
                    .build();

            NotificationManagerCompat notificationManager =
                    NotificationManagerCompat.from(this);
            notificationManager.notify(i + 1, notification);
        }
    }
}
```

Step 5: Create wearable activity class

The following `MainActivity.java` class is used for "wear" module. It renders the default created "activity_main.xml" layout file.

Listing 5-6 provides the main activity class. Note the code inline comments

Listing 5-6: MainActivity.java class

```java
package com.learning.android.notifications;

import android.app.Activity;
import android.app.Notification;
import android.os.Bundle;
import android.support.v4.app.NotificationCompat;
import android.support.v4.app.NotificationManagerCompat;
import android.support.wearable.view.WatchViewStub;
import android.widget.TextView;

import java.util.ArrayList;
import java.util.List;

// MainActivity.java
public class MainActivity extends Activity {

    private TextView mTextView;

    @Override
    protected void onCreate(Bundle savedInstanceState) {
        super.onCreate(savedInstanceState);
        setContentView(R.layout.activity_main);
        final WatchViewStub stub = (WatchViewStub)
                        findViewById(R.id.watch_view_stub);
        stub.setOnLayoutInflatedListener(new
                    WatchViewStub.OnLayoutInflatedListener() {

        @Override
        public void onLayoutInflated(WatchViewStub stub) {
                mTextView = (TextView) stub.findViewById(R.id.text);

                createNotifications();
            }
        });
    }

    // Method creates wearable notifications
    private void createNotifications() {
        List<String> titles = new ArrayList<String>();
        titles.add("Hello Android Mobile");
        titles.add("Hello Android Wear");
        titles.add("Hello Android TV");
        titles.add("Hello Android Tablet");

        for (int i = 0; i < titles.size(); i++) {
            // Shown in wear
            NotificationCompat.WearableExtender wearableExtender =
                new NotificationCompat.WearableExtender()
                    .setHintShowBackgroundOnly(true);

            // Shown in Handheld
            Notification notification = new
                    NotificationCompat.Builder(this)
                    .setSmallIcon(R.drawable.ic_launcher)
                    .setContentTitle(titles.get(i))
```

```
                    .setContentText("Learning Wearable notification."
                    + (i+1)).extend(wearableExtender)
                    .build();

            NotificationManagerCompat notificationManager =
                    NotificationManagerCompat.from(this);
            notificationManager.notify(i + 1, notification);
        }
    }
}
```

Step 6: Run the application in phone emulator

Select "mobile" option from drop down menu as shown in Figure 5-17. Run the mobile application. Select "mobile" option → click on Run.

Figure 5-17: Running mobile module

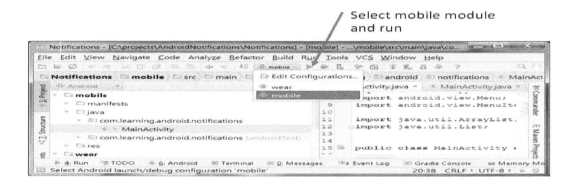

User can view the notifications on device lock screen as shown in Figure 5-18.

Figure 5-18: Material notifications on mobile lock screen

Step 5: Run the application in Watch emulator

Select "wear" option from drop down menu as shown in Figure 5-17. Run the wear application. Select "wear" option → click on Run.

User can view the notifications on wear emulator as shown in Figure 5-19.

Figure 5-19: Material notifications on wearable device

Material Themes

Tutorial 4: Using Material Themes for Status Bar and App Bar

The steps required to implement material themes for your status bar and app bar is listed below.

1. Create a custom theme for your application using material colors
2. Apply the theme to your application.

Step 1: Create a custom theme for your application using material colors.

Add the following elements to your "styles.xml" file. These material colors are supported only in Lollipop.

```
<resources>

    <style name="MyMaterialTheme" parent="GrayMaterialTheme.Base">
    </style>

    <style name="GrayMaterialTheme.Base"
            parent="Theme.AppCompat.Light.DarkActionBar">
```

```
        <item name="windowNoTitle">true</item>
        <item name="windowActionBar">false</item>
        <item name="colorPrimary">@color/material_grey_800</item>
        <item name="colorPrimaryDark">
            @color/primary_dark_material_dark</item>
        <item name="colorAccent">@color/material_grey_600</item>
    </style>

</resources>
```

Step 2: Apply the theme to your application.

Apply this theme to your application. Update the application manifest file. The "android.theme" attribute is used to add the newly created theme to your application.

```
<application
        android:allowBackup="true"
        android:icon="@mipmap/ic_launcher"
        android:label="@string/app_name"
        android:theme="@style/MyMaterialTheme">

        <activity>
            ...
        </activity>
</application>
```

Run the application, you can view the new material theme for your status bar and app bar as shown in Figure 5-20. Black color is used for status bar and gray color is used for app bar.

Figure 5-20: Material toolbar with menu icon and title

Material Animations

Tutorial 5: Implementing Material Animations

The following business scenario is implemented to demonstrate material animations.

Use Case Scenario:

- Design a main screen with "Linear Animation" and "Rotate Animation" buttons.
- Click on "Linear Animation" button. Show the linear animation on screen (Refer to Figure 5-21)
- Click on "Rotate Animation" button. Show the circular animation on screen (Refer to Figure 5-21)

The above described navigation scenario is shown in Figure 5-21.

Figure 5-21: Material animations – linear and circular

The steps required to implement the above-specified business scenario in Android are listed below:

1. Create a main activity layout file.
2. Create animation activity layout file.
3. Create Activity classes
4. Work on your configurations
5. Test the application.

The above-specified steps are described in the following sections:

Step 1: Create a main activity layout file

Here, reuse the previously created "activity_main.xml" file. Add the below provided button widgets.

Add the following button widget for translate animation.

```
<Button
    android:id="@+id/anim_linear"
    android:layout_width="250dp"
    android:layout_height="wrap_content"
    android:layout_marginBottom="5sp"
    android:layout_marginLeft="60dp"
    android:layout_marginRight="12dp"
    android:enabled="true"
    android:text="Linear Animation"
    android:onClick="ShowLinearAnimation"
    android:textSize="30sp" />
```

Add the following button widget for rotate animation.

```
<Button
    android:id="@+id/anim_rotate"
    android:layout_width="250dp"
    android:layout_height="wrap_content"
    android:layout_marginBottom="5sp"
    android:layout_marginLeft="60dp"
    android:layout_marginRight="12dp"
    android:enabled="true"
    android:text="Rotate Animation"
    android:onClick="showRotateAnimation"
    android:textSize="30sp" />
```

Step 2: Create an animation activity layout file

Go to res → layout → create "activity_animation_image.xml" file.

Create a layout file, and name the "activity_animation_image.xml". Add an "apple.jpeg" image to your "drawable" directory. The complete XML file is provided below.

```
<RelativeLayout xmlns:android=
    "http://schemas.android.com/apk/res/android"
    xmlns:tools="http://schemas.android.com/tools"
    android:layout_width="match_parent"
    android:layout_height="match_parent">

    <ImageView
        android:id="@+id/anim_apple"
        android:layout_width="wrap_content"
        android:layout_height="wrap_content"
        android:src="@drawable/apple"
        android:contentDescription="@null"/>

</RelativeLayout>
```

Step 3: Update main activity classes

Here, reuse the previously created main activity class. Add the following methods.

The following method receives the linear animation button click event.

```java
public void ShowLinearAnimation(View view) {
    Intent intent = new Intent(this, TranslateAnimationActivity.class);
    startActivity(intent);
}
```

The following method receives the rotate animation button click event.

```java
public void showRotateAnimation(View view) {
    Intent intent = new Intent(this, RotateAnimationActivity.class);
    startActivity(intent);
}
```

Step 4: Create animation activity classes

Create an activity class to display the linear image animation. Listing 5-7 provides the linear animation activity class code.

Listing 5-7: TranslateAnimationActivity.java class.

```java
package com.example.androidlearning.md;

import android.app.Activity;
import android.os.Bundle;
import android.util.Log;
import android.view.animation.Animation;
import android.view.animation.TranslateAnimation;
import android.widget.ImageView;

import com.example.androidlearning.R;

// TranslateAnimationActivity.java
public class TranslateAnimationActivity extends Activity {

    ImageView imageView = null;

    @Override
    protected void onCreate(Bundle savedInstanceState) {
        super.onCreate(savedInstanceState);
        setContentView(R.layout.activity_animation_image);

        // Loading the image
        imageView = (ImageView) findViewById(R.id.anim_apple);

        // Translating the image
        TranslateAnimation animation =
                new TranslateAnimation(0.0f, 400.0f, 0.0f, 0.0f);
        animation.setDuration(5000);
        animation.setRepeatCount(Animation.INFINITE);
        animation.setRepeatMode(2);
        animation.setFillAfter(true);
        imageView.startAnimation(animation);
    }
}
```

Create an activity class to show the rotate image animation. Listing 5-8 provides the rotate animation activity class code.

Listing 5-8: RotateAnimationActivity.java class.

```java
package com.example.androidlearning.md;

import android.app.Activity;
import android.os.Bundle;
import android.util.Log;
import android.view.animation.Animation;
import android.view.animation.LinearInterpolator;
import android.view.animation.RotateAnimation;
import android.widget.ImageView;

import com.example.androidlearning.R;

// RotateAnimationActivity.java
public class RotateAnimationActivity extends Activity {

    @Override
    protected void onCreate(Bundle savedInstanceState) {
        super.onCreate(savedInstanceState);
        setContentView(R.layout.activity_animation_image);

        // Rotating the image
        RotateAnimation anim =
                new RotateAnimation(0f, 350f, 350f, 700f);
        anim.setInterpolator(new LinearInterpolator());
        anim.setRepeatCount(Animation.INFINITE);
        anim.setDuration(700);

        // Loading the image for animation
        final ImageView androidImageView = (ImageView)
                findViewById(R.id.anim_apple);
        androidImageView.setAnimation(anim);
    }
}
```

Step 5: Work on your configurations

Add the above created activity classes to your application manifest file.

```xml
<activity android:name=".md.TranslateAnimationActivity"/>
<activity android:name=".md.RotateAnimationActivity"/>
```

Step 6: Test the application.

Follow the below provided step-by-step instructions to test the application.

1. Start the emulator
2. Click on application Icon → Main screen will be shown with "Linear Animation" and "Rotate Animation" buttons (Refer to Figure 5-21)
3. Click on "Linear Animation" button (Refer to Figure 5-21)
4. User can view the translate animation screen.
5. Click on "Rotate Animation" button (Refer to Figure 5-21)
6. User can view the rotate animation screen.

View Shadows

Tutorial 6: UI elements with elevation attribute

Material design introduces elevation for UI elements. In addition to X and Y properties, Android introduces Z -property for UI elements. Z -property represents the elevation view.

An example use of elevation attribute is provided below.

```
<LinearLayout
        android:layout_width="match_parent"
        android:layout_height="wrap_content"
        android:layout_gravity="center_horizontal"
        android:orientation="vertical">

        <TextView
            android:layout_width="wrap_content"
            android:layout_height="wrap_content"
            android:background="@drawable/rectangle"
            android:text="Hallo World"
            android:padding="8dp"
            android:elevation="75dp" />

</LinearLayout>
```

Use the below provided "rectangle.xml" file.

```
<?xml version="1.0" encoding="utf-8"?>
<shape xmlns:android="http://schemas.android.com/apk/res/android"
    android:shape="rectangle">
    <solid android:color="#0073ff" />
    <corners android:radius="16dp" />
</shape>
```

Run the application to view the output on screen.

Summary

This section summarizes the material design widgets. Figure 5-22 summarizes the most important points described in this chapter.

- Material design is a specification and set of guidelines for developing visual, motion, interactive, and animation effects in your application.
- The minimum required target SDK for material design is API 21
- The Android v7 support library provides widgets for developing material design applications.
- Notifications has undergone visual changes to support evolving material design specifications. A notification will have four attributes: icon, title, description, and time stamp.
- The material toolbar activity class must extend the `AppCompatActivity` class.
- Material design introduces an elevation property for UI elements. In addition to X and Y properties, Android introduces a Z property for UI elements.

- The material toolbar is a UI element that can contain icons, images, and menus.
- Cards and recycler view widgets are used to display collection of data objects.

Figure 5-22 Material design components

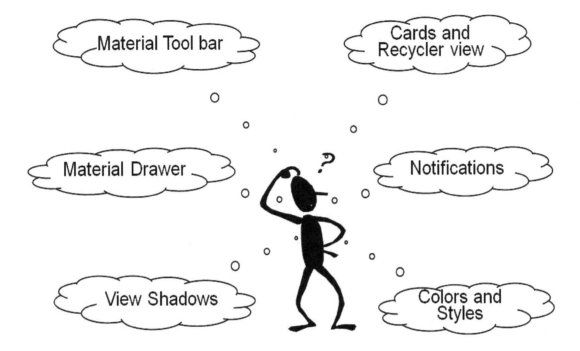

Chapter 6. Data Persistence in Android

Mobile databases are used to store simple and light-weight data. The data will be stored in the device file system. Traditional relational databases contain a SQL engine that runs as a separate system process. Mobile databases does not contain a SQL engine, and will not run as a process. Instead they store the data to a file and read from the file. The volume of the data storage is limited. In general, mobile databases are used to store application-specific data, not designed to store the business transactional data.

Don't expect database clustering, automatic failover, and data replication features in mobile databases. Mobile databases are not designed to compete with relational databases. Mobile database do not require any JDBC, ODBC bridge to access the stored data. Android provides a simple API to persist and read data from the file system. The JDK-provided "file-io" API can also be used to read and save the data.

The commonly used mobile data persistence frameworks are listed below.

- SQLite
- Realm IO
- Shared Preferences Object (SPO)
- File IO (JDK)
- Green DAO
- ORMLite
- Core Data

All of the preceding frameworks provide the same functionality, though they do so using different techniques; all are used for persisting the data in mobile devices. This chapter illustrates the complete use of SQLite, Realm IO, File-IO, and the Shared Preferences Object.

This chapter will discuss the following topics:

- Commonly used mobile data persistence frameworks
- How to store the data in Android applications using SQLite
- How to store the data in Android applications using Realm IO
- How to store the data in Android applications using File IO
- How to store the data in Android applications using the Shared Preferences Object
- How to use database persistence frameworks in Android application development
- How to execute select, insert, delete, and update statements

Anatomy of Android Databases

SQLite

SQLite is an open-source light weight embedded mobile database. This is the default database packaged with the Android platform. Android developers don't have to use the JDBC and ODBC API to access the database. Android-provides helper classes that can be used to access the data stored in the device's file system. Applications use "android.database.sqlite" package classes to manage device's own private database. SQLite follows a JDBC-style programming model. Developers has to map the data returned from the resultset to the domain objects. Overall, SQLite provides simple, flexible, and easy to learn API for building SQL statements.

The following code is used to query the data from a table. The following code fetches all the records from the "contacts" table.

```
Cursor result = db.rawQuery("select * from contacts", null);
result.moveToFirst();
```

The above code is equivalent to the following SQL statement.

```
Select * from contacts;
```

The following code is used for deleting an existing record.

```
Integer id = 123;
SQLiteDatabase db = this.getWritableDatabase();
int rowsDeleted = db.delete("contacts",
                "id = ? ",
                new String[] { Integer.toString(id) });
```

The above code is equivalent to the following SQL statement.

```
delete from contacts where id = '1234';
```

The following code is used for inserting a new record.

```
SQLiteDatabase db = this.getWritableDatabase();
ContentValues contentValues = new ContentValues();
contentValues.put("firstName", firstName);
contentValues.put("lastName", lastName);
contentValues.put("email", email);
contentValues.put("street", street);
contentValues.put("zip", zip);

// Returns the inserted Primary Key value
Long id = db.insert("contacts", null, contentValues);
```

The above code is equivalent to the following SQL statement; note that in SQLite the value of the primary key (id) is auto-generated.

```
insert into
contacts(firstName, lastName, email, street, zip)
values ("John", "Smith", "js@test.com", "Roundabout", "65892");
```

The following is used to delete an existing table.

```
db.execSQL("DROP TABLE IF EXISTS contacts");
onCreate(db);
```

The above code is equivalent to the following SQL statement.

```
drop table contacts;
```

The following code is used to create a new table.

```
db.execSQL(" create table contacts " +
        " (id integer primary key, firstName text,
            lastName text, email text, street text, zip text)");
```

The above code is equivalent to the following SQL statement.

```
CREATE TABLE contacts (
    id int NOT NULL,
    firstName varchar(255),
    lastName varchar(255),
    email varchar(255),
    street varchar(255),
    zip varchar(255),
    PRIMARY KEY (id)
);
```

Realm IO

Realm IO is an open-source object-relational mobile database. This framework uses object-relational (OR) mapping technique. OR mapping is a very popular database layer programming model in Java enterprise application development. In this model domain objects are mapped to database entities. JPA, Hibernate, and Toplink are some of the commonly used OR mapping frameworks in the Java landscape. Realm IO provides the similar a programming technique for mobile data persistence. This framework can be used an alternative to the SQLite database.

Ream IO supports the boolean, short, int, long, float, double, String, Date, and byte[] data types. All write transactions (write, delete, and update) must be wrapped inside a transaction. An example code is provide below.

```
// Begins the transaction
realm.beginTransaction();

// ... Do your add, remove, and updates here

// Commit the transaction
realm.commitTransaction();
```

The following code is used for querying the data; fetching the matched records from a table.

```
RealmResults<Contacts> query = realm.where(Contacts.class).findAll();
```

This code is equivalent to the following SQL statement.

```
select * from contacts;
```

Realm IO supports the following "where" conditions.

* equalTo() and notEqualTo()
* between, greaterThan(), lessThan(), greaterThanOrEqualTo(), and lessThanOrEqualTo()
* contains(), beginsWith(), and endsWith()

An example use of `equalTo()` is provided below. The following code is used for querying and filtering the data.

```
RealmResults<Contacts> result2 = realm.where(Contacts.class)
            .equalTo("firstName", "John")
            .or()
            .equalTo("firstName", "Jason")
            .findAll();
```

This code is equivalent to the following SQL statement.

```
select * from contacts where firstName = 'John' OR firstName = 'Jason';
```

Similarly, the following code uses multiple conditions in its "where" clause. The `beginGroup()` is equivalent to a left parentheses and `endGroup()` is equivalent to a right parentheses. An example code is provided below.

```
RealmResults<Contacts> r =
        realm.where(Contacts.class)
        .greaterThan("id", 0)   //implicit AND
        .beginGroup()   // Left parentheses
            .equalTo("name", "John")
            .or()
            .contains("name", "Jason")
        .endGroup()   // Right parentheses
        .findAll();
```

This code is equivalent to the following SQL statement.

```
select * from contacts where id > 0 AND (firstName = 'John' OR firstName = 'Jason');
```

The following example provides the sorted output.

```
RealmResults<Contacts> result = realm.where(Contacts.class).findAll();
RealmResults<Contacts> sortedDescending =
        result.sort("firstName", RealmResults.SORT_ORDER_DECENDING);
```

This code is equivalent to the following SQL statement.

```
select * from contacts order by firstName desc;
```

Unless you explicitly specify otherwise, the default sorting is ascending. An example code is provided below.

```
RealmResults<Contacts> result = realm.where(Contacts.class).findAll();
RealmResults<Contacts> sortedDescending = result.sort("firstName");
```

This code is equivalent to the following SQL statement.

```
select * from contacts order by firstName asc;
```

The following code is used to insert a new record into the table.

```
Realm realm = Realm.getInstance(getApplicationContext());

// Begings the transaction
realm.beginTransaction();
Contacts contacts = realm.createObject(Contacts.class);

// Adding Primary Key
contacts.setId(UUID.randomUUID().toString());
contacts.setFirstName(firstName);
contacts.setLastName(lastName);
contacts.setEmail(emailId);
contacts.setStreet(streetName);
contacts.setZip(zipCode);

// Commit the transaction
realm.commitTransaction();
```

This code is equivalent to the following SQL statement.

```
insert into
contacts(id, firstName, lastName, emailId, streetName, zipCode)
values ("123", "John", "Smith", "js@test.com", "Roundabout", "65892");
```

The following code is used to delete an existing record from the table.

```
Realm realm = Realm.getInstance(getApplicationContext());
realm.beginTransaction();

RealmResults<Contacts> results = realm.where(Contacts.class).findAll();

results.remove(0);
realm.commitTransaction();
```

Similarly, the following code is used to update an existing record.

```
Realm realm = Realm.getInstance(getApplicationContext());
realm.beginTransaction();

RealmResults<Contacts> results = realm.where(Contacts.class).findAll();

Contacts contact = results.get(0);
contact.setLastName("New Name");
realm.commitTransaction();
```

Shared Preferences Object

Android provides the `SharedPreferences` interface, which is used to modify the data stored in a shared preferences object. As with Java's `Map` interface, this object can be used to store both key and value data. This object can be used to save preferences data and retrieve it as needed in your application. Various `put(...)` and `get(...)` methods are available to save and read data from the preferences object. This approach is more suitable for storing simple light-weight data without having any entity relationships.

The below provided `commit()` or `apply()` methods are used to commit the code into a shared preferences object. An example code is provided below.

```
SharedPreferences preferences =
            PreferenceManager.getDefaultSharedPreferences(this);
SharedPreferences.Editor editor = preferences.edit();
editor.putString("username", "Srinivas");
editor.putString("password", "admin123");
editor.commit();
```

The following `remove()` method is used to remove saved data from the shared preferences object.

```
editor.remove("username");
editor.commit();
```

Similarly, the below provided `clear()` method is used to remove all values from a preferences object.

```
editor.clear();
editor.commit();
```

File IO

The `java.io` package defines classes and interfaces to access files, file attributes, and file systems. Android supports the JDK-provided "file-io" API for reading and writing data streams.

SQLite

SQLite stores data in a file system on your device. We don't have to use a relational database framework like JDBC or ODBC to access the database. We can use the default helper classes provided with Android to access the data stored in the device's file system. The following tutorial will help you to understand the Android SQLite API, which is used for implementing database operations such as create, insert, delete, update, and so forth.

Tutorial 1: Create, Read, Update, and Delete operations

The following business scenario is implemented using SQLite database.

Use Case Scenario:

- Design a main screen with "SQLite" button.
- Click on "SQLite" button. User navigates to the next (user data) screen.
- Design and create a user interface with first name, last name, email, street, and zip code
- Add "Save", "Delete" buttons.
- Enter data and click on "Save" button.
- User entered data will be inserted into the database.
- Similarly, user can read, update, and delete data from database.

The above described scenario is shown in Figure 6-1.

Figure 6-1: Main and navigation screens

The steps required to implement the above-specified business scenario in Android using SQLite database are listed below:

1. Create a layout file.
2. Create Activity classes
3. Create a POJO class
4. Create a database helper class
5. Test the application.

The above-specified steps are described in the following sections:

Step 1: Create a layout file

Go to res → layout → create "activity_main.xml" layout file.

The following "activity_main.xml" file is used to create the main screen.

```
<RelativeLayout xmlns:android =
    "http://schemas.android.com/apk/res/android"
    xmlns:tools="http://schemas.android.com/tools"
    android:layout_width="match_parent"
    android:layout_height="match_parent"
    android:paddingLeft="@dimen/activity_horizontal_margin"
    android:paddingRight="@dimen/activity_horizontal_margin"
    android:paddingTop="@dimen/activity_vertical_margin"
    android:paddingBottom="@dimen/activity_vertical_margin"
    tools:context=".MainActivity">

    <LinearLayout
        android:layout_width="match_parent"
        android:layout_height="wrap_content"
        android:layout_gravity="center_horizontal"
```

```
                    android:orientation="vertical">

            <Button
                    android:id="@+id/sqlite_button"
                    android:layout_width="200dp"
                    android:layout_height="wrap_content"
                    android:layout_marginBottom="5sp"
                    android:layout_marginLeft="60dp"
                    android:layout_marginRight="12dp"
                    android:enabled="true"
                    android:text="SQLite"
                    android:textSize="30sp"/>

        </LinearLayout>
</RelativeLayout>
```

Go to res → layout → create "activity_sqlite.xml" layout file.

The following "activity_sqlite.xml" file is used to create the navigation (user data) screen. This layout shows the user specific attributes such as first name, last name, email, and so forth.

```
<RelativeLayout xmlns:android=
        "http://schemas.android.com/apk/res/android"
        xmlns:tools="http://schemas.android.com/tools"
        android:layout_width="match_parent"
        android:layout_height="match_parent"
        android:paddingLeft="@dimen/activity_horizontal_margin"
        android:paddingRight="@dimen/activity_horizontal_margin"
        android:paddingTop="@dimen/activity_vertical_margin"
        android:paddingBottom="@dimen/activity_vertical_margin"
        tools:context=".MainActivity">

        <LinearLayout
                android:layout_width="match_parent"
                android:layout_height="wrap_content"
                android:layout_gravity="center_horizontal"
                android:orientation="vertical">

            <TextView
                    android:layout_width="match_parent"
                    android:layout_height="wrap_content"
                    android:layout_marginTop="5dp"
                    android:enabled="true"
                    android:text="@string/first_name" />

            <EditText
                    android:id="@+id/fname_edittext"
                    android:layout_width="match_parent"
                    android:layout_height="wrap_content"
                    android:layout_marginTop="5dp"
                    android:enabled="true"
                    android:textSize="30sp" />

            <TextView
                    android:layout_width="match_parent"
```

```
            android:layout_height="wrap_content"
            android:layout_marginTop="5dp"
            android:enabled="true"
            android:text="@string/last_name" />

        <EditText
            android:id="@+id/lname_edittext"
            android:layout_width="match_parent"
            android:layout_height="wrap_content"
            android:layout_marginTop="5dp"
            android:enabled="true"
            android:textSize="30sp" />

        <TextView
            android:layout_width="match_parent"
            android:layout_height="wrap_content"
            android:layout_marginTop="5dp"
            android:enabled="true"
            android:text="Email " />

        <EditText
            android:id="@+id/email"
            android:layout_width="match_parent"
            android:layout_height="wrap_content"
            android:layout_marginTop="5dp"
            android:enabled="true"
            android:textSize="30sp" />

        <TextView
            android:layout_width="match_parent"
            android:layout_height="wrap_content"
            android:layout_marginTop="5dp"
            android:enabled="true"
            android:text="Street " />

        <EditText
            android:id="@+id/street"
            android:layout_width="match_parent"
            android:layout_height="wrap_content"
            android:layout_marginTop="5dp"
            android:enabled="true"
            android:textSize="30sp" />

        <TextView
            android:layout_width="match_parent"
            android:layout_height="wrap_content"
            android:layout_marginTop="5dp"
            android:enabled="true"
            android:text="Zip Code " />

        <EditText
            android:id="@+id/zip"
            android:layout_width="match_parent"
            android:layout_height="wrap_content"
            android:layout_marginTop="5dp"
            android:enabled="true"
            android:textSize="30sp"/>
```

```xml
<Button
    android:id="@+id/save_button"
    android:layout_width="200dp"
    android:layout_height="wrap_content"
    android:layout_marginBottom="5sp"
    android:layout_marginLeft="60dp"
    android:layout_marginRight="12dp"
    android:enabled="true"
    android:text="@string/save"
    android:textSize="30sp" />

<Button
    android:id="@+id/delete_button"
    android:layout_width="200dp"
    android:layout_height="wrap_content"
    android:layout_marginBottom="5sp"
    android:layout_marginLeft="60dp"
    android:layout_marginRight="12dp"
    android:enabled="true"
    android:text="Delete"
    android:textSize="30sp" />

    </LinearLayout>
</RelativeLayout>
```

Step 2: Create Activity classes

The following `MainActivity.java` class is used to create the main screen with "SQLite" button. This class renders the previously created "activity_main.xml" file.

Listing 6-4 provides the main activity class. Note the code inline comments.

Listing 6-4: MainActivity.java class.

```java
package com.example.androidlearning;

import android.app.Activity;
import android.content.Intent;
import android.os.Bundle;
import android.view.Menu;
import android.view.MenuItem;
import android.view.View;
import android.widget.Button;

import com.example.androidlearning.db.SQLiteActivity;

// MainActivity.java
public class MainActivity extends Activity {

    @Override
    protected void onCreate(Bundle savedInstanceState) {
        super.onCreate(savedInstanceState);
        setContentView(R.layout.activity_main);

        // Button event listener to capture the click event
        Button sqliteButton =(Button) findViewById(R.id.sqlite_button);
```

```
        sqliteButton.setEnabled(true);
        sqliteButton.setOnClickListener(saveButtonListener);
    }

    // Create an anonymous class to act as a button click listener
    private View.OnClickListener saveButtonListener = new
    View.OnClickListener() {
        public void onClick(View v) {
            showSQLiteDataScreen();
        }
    };

    // Calling to user data scren
    private void showSQLiteDataScreen() {
        Intent intent = new Intent(this, SQLiteActivity.class);
        startActivity(intent);
    }
}
```

The following `SQLiteActivity.java` class is used to create the user data screen with "Save" and "Delete" buttons. This class renders the previously created "activity_sqlite.xml" file.

Listing 6-5 provides the SQLite activity class. Note the code inline comments.

Listing 6-5: SQLiteActivity.java class.

```
package com.example.androidlearning.db;

import android.app.Activity;
import android.os.Bundle;
import android.util.Log;
import android.view.View;
import android.widget.Button;
import android.widget.EditText;

import com.example.androidlearning.R;

import java.util.ArrayList;

// SQLiteActivity.java
public class SQLiteActivity extends Activity  {

    @Override
    protected void onCreate(Bundle savedInstanceState) {
        super.onCreate(savedInstanceState);
        setContentView(R.layout.activity_sqlite);

        // Save button listener to capture the click event
        Button saveButton = (Button) findViewById(R.id.save_button);
        saveButton.setEnabled(true);
        saveButton.setOnClickListener(saveDataListener);
    }

    // Capture's the Saves button click event
    private View.OnClickListener saveDataListener = new
        View.OnClickListener() {
        public void onClick(View v) {
```

```
            EditText fname = (EditText)
                    findViewById(R.id.fname_edittext);
            EditText lname = (EditText)
                    findViewById(R.id.lname_edittext);
            EditText email = (EditText) findViewById(R.id.email);
            EditText street = (EditText) findViewById(R.id.street);
            EditText zip = (EditText) findViewById(R.id.zip);

            String firstName = fname.getText().toString();
            String lastName = lname.getText().toString();
            String emailId = email.getText().toString();
            String streetName = street.getText().toString();
            String zipCode = zip.getText().toString();

            saveData(firstName, lastName, emailId,streetName, zipCode);
        }
    };

    // Calling DBHelper class methods.
    public void saveData(String firstName, String lastName,
                String email, String street, String zip) {
        DBHelper dbHelper = new DBHelper(this);

        // Inserting a new record.
        Long id = dbHelper.insertContact(firstName, lastName, email,
                    street, zip);
        System.out.println("------ id -----" + id);

        // Finding out the row count
        int rows = dbHelper.numberOfRows();
        System.out.println("------ rows -----" + rows);

        // Reading data from a table
        ArrayList<ContactsDTO> contactsList =
                        dbHelper.getContactsList();
        System.out.println (" Size: " contactsList.size());
        for(ContactsDTO contactsDTO : contactsList) {
            System.out.println(contactsDTO);
        }
    }
}
```

Step 3: Create a POJO class

The below provided POJO class is used to store the data.

```
package com.example.androidlearning.db;

// ContactsDTO.java
public class ContactsDTO {

    private Integer id;
    private String firstName;
    private String lastName;
    private String email;
    private String street;
```

```
        private String zip;

        // Add getter and setter methods

        @Override
        public String toString() {
            StringBuilder result = new StringBuilder();
            String NEW_LINE = System.getProperty("line.separator");

            result.append(" name:    " + firstName + NEW_LINE);
            result.append(" email : " + email + NEW_LINE);
            result.append(" street :   " + street + NEW_LINE);
            result.append(" zip : " + zip + NEW_LINE);
            result.append(" id : "  + id + NEW_LINE);

            result.append("}");
            return result.toString();
        }
    }
```

Step 4: Create a database helper class

The `DBHelper.java` is a utility class which contains create, insert, delete, and update operations. These operations can be re-used by any other activity classes. This `DBHelper` class must extend the Android-provided `SQLiteOpenHelper` class. An example implementation is provided below.

```
public class DBHelper extends SQLiteOpenHelper {
    ...
}
```

The below-provided `onCreaate()` method creates a new table.

```
public void onCreate(SQLiteDatabase db) {
    db.execSQL(
        " create table contacts " +
        " (id integer primary key, firstName text, lastName text,
            email text, street text, zip text)"
    );
}
```

The below-provided `onUpgrade()` method drops an existing table.

```
public void onUpgrade(SQLiteDatabase db,int oldVersion, int newVersion) {
    db.execSQL("DROP TABLE IF EXISTS contacts");
    onCreate(db);
}
```

The below-provided code is used to obtain the writable database connection.

```
SQLiteDatabase db = this.getWritableDatabase();
```

The below-provided code is used to obtain the readable database connection.

```
SQLiteDatabase db = this.getReadableDatabase();
```

The below-provided code is used for counting the number of rows in a table.

```
public int numberOfRows() {
    SQLiteDatabase db = this.getReadableDatabase();
    int numRows = (int) DatabaseUtils.queryNumEntries(db,
                        CONTACTS_TABLE_NAME);
    return numRows;
}
```

The below-provided method obtains the existing rows of a table. The returned cursor encapsulates the complete resultset.

```
public Cursor getData(int id) {
    SQLiteDatabase db = this.getReadableDatabase();
    Cursor res = db.rawQuery( "select * from contacts where id="+id+"",
                        null );
    return res;
}
```

The following method deletes a matched record. Here, the primary key "id" is used to delete a record from the table.

```
public Integer deleteContact(Integer id) {
    SQLiteDatabase db = this.getWritableDatabase();
    return db.delete("contacts", "id = ? ",
            new String[] { Integer.toString(id) });
}
```

Similarly, the following method obtains the records from a table.

```
public ArrayList<ContactsDTO> getContactsList() {
    ArrayList<ContactsDTO> contactsList = new ArrayList<ContactsDTO>();
    SQLiteDatabase db = this.getReadableDatabase();
    Cursor res =  db.rawQuery("select * from contacts", null);
    res.moveToFirst();

    while(res.isAfterLast() == false){
        ContactsDTO contactsDTO = new ContactsDTO();
        String fname = res.getString(res.getColumnIndex("firstName"));
        String lname = res.getString(res.getColumnIndex("lastName"));
        String email = res.getString(res.getColumnIndex("email"));
        String street = res.getString(res.getColumnIndex("street"));
        String zip = res.getString(res.getColumnIndex("zip"));
        Integer id = res.getInt(res.getColumnIndex("id"));

        contactsDTO.setFirstName(fname);
        contactsDTO.setLastName(lname);
        contactsDTO.setEmail(email);
        contactsDTO.setStreet(street);
        contactsDTO.setZip(zip);
        contactsDTO.setId(id);

        contactsList.add(contactsDTO);
        res.moveToNext();
    }
```

```
        return contactsList;
}
```

Listing 6-6 provides the complete class code. Note the code inline comments.

Listing 6-6: DBHelper.java class.

```java
package com.example.androidlearning.db;

import android.content.ContentValues;
import android.content.Context;
import android.database.Cursor;
import android.database.DatabaseUtils;
import android.database.sqlite.SQLiteDatabase;
import android.database.sqlite.SQLiteOpenHelper;

import java.util.ArrayList;

// DBHelper.java
public class DBHelper extends SQLiteOpenHelper {

    public static final String DATABASE_NAME = "TestDB.db";
    public static final Integer DATABASE_VERSION = 1;
    public static final String CONTACTS_TABLE_NAME = "contacts";
    public static final String CONTACTS_COLUMN_FNAME = "firstName";
    public static final String CONTACTS_COLUMN_LNAME = "lastName";

    public DBHelper(Context context) {
        super(context, DATABASE_NAME, null, DATABASE_VERSION);
    }

    // Creating a table
    @Override
    public void onCreate(SQLiteDatabase db) {
        db.execSQL(
            " create table contacts " +
            " (id integer primary key, firstName text, lastName text,
                    email text, street text, zip text)"
        );
    }

    // Droping a table
    @Override
    public void onUpgrade(SQLiteDatabase db, int oldVersion,
            int newVersion) {
        db.execSQL("DROP TABLE IF EXISTS contacts");
        onCreate(db);
    }

    // Inserting a new record into a table
    public Long insertContact(String firstName, String lastName,
            String email, String street, String zip) {
        SQLiteDatabase db = this.getWritableDatabase();
        ContentValues contentValues = new ContentValues();
        contentValues.put("firstName", firstName);
        contentValues.put("lastName", lastName);
        contentValues.put("email", email);
```

```java
        contentValues.put("street", street);
        contentValues.put("zip", zip);

        // Returns the inserted Primary Key value
        Long id = db.insert("contacts", null, contentValues);
        return id;
    }

    // Reading the data from a table
    public Cursor getData(int id) {
        SQLiteDatabase db = this.getReadableDatabase();
        Cursor res =  db.rawQuery( "select * from contacts where
                            id="+id+"", null );
        return res;
    }

    // Counting the number of rows in a table
    public int numberOfRows() {
        SQLiteDatabase db = this.getReadableDatabase();
        int numRows = (int) DatabaseUtils.queryNumEntries(db,
                    CONTACTS_TABLE_NAME);
        return numRows;
    }

    // Updating a table row data
    public boolean updateContact(Integer id, String firstName,
        String lastName, String email, String street, String zip) {
        SQLiteDatabase db = this.getWritableDatabase();
        ContentValues contentValues = new ContentValues();
        contentValues.put("firstName", firstName);
        contentValues.put("lastName", lastName);
        contentValues.put("email", email);
        contentValues.put("street", street);
        contentValues.put("zip", zip);

        db.update("contacts", contentValues, "id = ?",
                    new String[] { Integer.toString(id) } );
        return true;
    }

    // Deleting a table row
    public Integer deleteContact(Integer id) {
        SQLiteDatabase db = this.getWritableDatabase();
        return db.delete("contacts", "id = ? ",
                new String[] { Integer.toString(id) });
    }

    // Obtaining list of rows of a table
    public ArrayList<ContactsDTO> getContactsList() {
        ArrayList<ContactsDTO> contactsList =
                        new ArrayList<ContactsDTO>();
        SQLiteDatabase db = this.getReadableDatabase();
        Cursor res =  db.rawQuery("select * from contacts", null);
        res.moveToFirst();

        while(res.isAfterLast() == false){
            ContactsDTO contactsDTO = new ContactsDTO();
```

```
String fname =
    res.getString(res.getColumnIndex("firstName"));
String lname =
    res.getString(res.getColumnIndex(("lastName"));
String email = res.getString(res.getColumnIndex("email"));
String street =res.getString(res.getColumnIndex("street"));
String zip = res.getString(res.getColumnIndex("zip"));
Integer id = res.getInt(res.getColumnIndex("id"));

contactsDTO.setFirstName(fname);
contactsDTO.setLastName(lname);
contactsDTO.setEmail(email);
contactsDTO.setStreet(street);
contactsDTO.setZip(zip);
contactsDTO.setId(id);

contactsList.add(contactsDTO);
res.moveToNext();
    }

    return contactsList;
    }
}
```

Step 5: Test the application.

Follow the below provided step-by-step instructions to test the application.

1. Start the emulator
2. Click on application Icon → Main screen will be displayed with "SQLite" button
3. Click on "SQLite" button
4. User data screen will be shown (Refer to Figure 6-1)
5. Enter the data → click on "Save" button.
6. User entered data will be saved.
7. You can view the inserted records on the console.

Similarly, add the "Update" and "Delete" buttons to the user data screen. Capture the button events in SQLiteActivity class to test the update and delete functionality.

Advantages

- The data is stored into a single database file.
- The SQLite file format is cross-platform; data can be copied from one machine to another.
- No additional database engine is required. The data is stored in a single file on the device.
- The SQLite programming model is syntactically similar to the SQL programming model, and provides support for create, update, read, and insert statements.
- In SQLite, the value of the primary key is auto-generated.

Limitations

- SQLite does not support the object-relational mapping technique. The developer must map the domain objects to database entities.

- Limited file size.

Realm IO for Android

The following tutorial will help you to understand the Android Realm API, which is used to implement database operations such as create, insert, delete, update, and so forth.

Tutorial 2: Create, Read, Update, and Delete operations

Figure 6-2: Main and navigation screens

The following business scenario is implemented in Android using Realm database.

Use Case Scenario:

- Design a main screen with "Ream IO" button.
- Click on "Ream IO" button. User navigates to the next (user data) screen.
- Design and create a user interface with first name, last name, email, street, and zip code
- Add "Save", "Delete" buttons.
- Enter data → click on "Save" button.
- User entered data will be inserted into the database.
- Similarly, user can perform the read, update, and delete operations.

The above described navigation scenario is shown in Figure 6-2.

The steps required to implement the above-specified business scenario using Realm API are listed below:

1. Create a layout file.
2. Create Activity classes
3. Create a POJO class
4. Create a database helper class
5. Test the application.

The above-specified steps are described in the following sections:

Step 1: Create a layout file

Here, reuse the previously created "activity_main.xml" file. Add the following button element to the main layout file.

```
<Button
        android:id="@+id/realm_button"
        android:layout_width="200dp"
        android:layout_height="wrap_content"
        android:layout_marginBottom="5sp"
        android:layout_marginLeft="60dp"
        android:layout_marginRight="12dp"
        android:enabled="true"
        android:text="Realm"
        android:textSize="30sp"/>
```

The following layout "activity_realm.xml" file is used to create the navigation (user data) screen. This layout shows the user specific attributes such as first name, last name, email, and so forth. Here, reuse the elements created in "activity_sqlite.xml" file. An example code is provided below.

```
<RelativeLayout xmlns:android=
        "http://schemas.android.com/apk/res/android"
        xmlns:tools="http://schemas.android.com/tools"
        android:layout_width="match_parent"
        android:layout_height="match_parent"
        android:paddingLeft="@dimen/activity_horizontal_margin"
        android:paddingRight="@dimen/activity_horizontal_margin"
        android:paddingTop="@dimen/activity_vertical_margin"
        android:paddingBottom="@dimen/activity_vertical_margin"
        tools:context=".MainActivity">

    ...

    <Button
        android:id="@+id/realm_save_button"
        android:layout_width="200dp"
        android:layout_height="wrap_content"
        android:layout_marginBottom="5sp"
        android:layout_marginLeft="60dp"
        android:layout_marginRight="12dp"
        android:enabled="true"
        android:text="@string/save"
        android:textSize="30sp" />

</RelativeLayout>
```

Step 2: Create Activity classes

Here, reuse the `MainActivity.java` created in Tutorial -1. Add the following lines of code to the `onCreate()` method of `MainActivity.java` class.

```
Button realmButton = (Button) findViewById(R.id.realm_button);
realmButton.setEnabled(true);
realmButton.setOnClickListener(realmButtonListener);
```

The above code captures the "Realm" button click event. Add the following methods to `MainActivity.java` class to receive the button click event.

```
// Receive's save button click event
private View.OnClickListener realmButtonListener = new
View.OnClickListener() {
    public void onClick(View v) {
        showRealmDataScreen();
    }
};

// Calling user data screen
private void showRealmDataScreen() {
Intent intent = new Intent(this, RealmActivity.class);
    startActivity(intent);
}
```

The following `RealmActivity.java` class renders the user data screen with "Save" button. It uses the previously created "activity_realm.xml" layout file.

Listing 6-1 provides the Realm activity class. Note the code inline comments.

Listing 6-1: RealmActivity.java class.

```
package com.example.androidlearning.db;

import android.app.Activity;
import android.os.Bundle;
import android.util.Log;
import android.view.View;
import android.widget.Button;
import android.widget.EditText;
import com.example.androidlearning.R;
import java.util.ArrayList;
import java.util.UUID;
import io.realm.Realm;
import io.realm.RealmResults;

// RealmActivity.java
public class RealmActivity extends Activity {

    @Override
    protected void onCreate(Bundle savedInstanceState) {
        super.onCreate(savedInstanceState);
        setContentView(R.layout.activity_realm);

        Button saveButton=(Button)findViewById(R.id.realm_save_button);
```

```
        saveButton.setEnabled(true);
        saveButton.setOnClickListener(saveDataListener);
}

private View.OnClickListener saveDataListener = new
View.OnClickListener() {
    public void onClick(View v) {
        // Inserting a new record
        addContact();

        // Reading data from table
        ArrayList<Contacts> contacts = getContacts();

        // Updating the record
        updateContact();

        // Deleting a record.
        //deleteContact();
    }
};

// Reading data from table
private ArrayList<Contacts> getContacts() {
    ArrayList<Contacts> contactsList = new ArrayList<>();
    Realm realm = Realm.getInstance(this);
    RealmResults<Contacts> query =
        realm.where(Contacts.class).findAll();
    for (Contacts contact : query) {
        contactsList.add(contact);
        System.out.println("---- name -----" + contact.toString());
    }
    System.out.println("------ query -----" + query.size());
    return contactsList;
}

// Inserting a new record
public void addContact() {
    Realm realm = Realm.getInstance(getApplicationContext());

    // Beings the transaction
    realm.beginTransaction();
    Contacts contacts = realm.createObject(Contacts.class);

    EditText fname = (EditText) findViewById(R.id.fname_edittext);
    EditText lname = (EditText) findViewById(R.id.lname_edittext);
    EditText email = (EditText) findViewById(R.id.email);
    EditText street = (EditText) findViewById(R.id.street);
    EditText zip = (EditText) findViewById(R.id.zip);

    String firstName = fname.getText().toString();
    String lastName = lname.getText().toString();
    String emailId = email.getText().toString();
    String streetName = street.getText().toString();
    String zipCode = zip.getText().toString();

    // Adding Primary Key
    contacts.setId(UUID.randomUUID().toString());
```

```
        contacts.setFirstName(firstName);
        contacts.setLastName(lastName);
        contacts.setEmail(emailId);
        contacts.setStreet(streetName);
        contacts.setZip(zipCode);
        System.out.println("--- contacts ---" + contacts.toString());

        // Commit the transaction
        realm.commitTransaction();
    }

    // Deleting a record.
    private void deleteContact() {
        Realm realm = Realm.getInstance(getApplicationContext());
        realm.beginTransaction();

        RealmResults<Contacts> results =
                realm.where(Contacts.class).findAll();

        results.remove(0);
        realm.commitTransaction();
    }

    // Updating the data
    private void updateContact() {
        Realm realm = Realm.getInstance(getApplicationContext());
        realm.beginTransaction();

        RealmResults<Contacts> results =
                realm.where(Contacts.class).findAll();

        Contacts contact = results.get(0);
        contact.setLastName("New Name");
        realm.commitTransaction();
    }
}
```

Step 3: Create a POJO class

The below provided POJO class is used to store the data. This POJO class must extend the `RealmObject`. POJO class must contain only getter and setter methods.

```
package com.example.androidlearning.db;

// Contacts.java
public class Contacts extends RealmObject {

    private String id;
    private String firstName;
    private String lastName;
    private String email;
    private String street;
    private String zip;

    // Add getter and setter methods
```

}

Step 4: Test the application.

Follow the below provided step-by-step instructions to test the application.

1. Start the emulator
2. Click on application Icon → Main screen will be displayed with "Realm" button
3. Click on "Realm" button
4. User data screen will be shown (Refer to Figure 6-2)
5. Enter the data → click on "Save" button.
6. User entered data will be saved.
7. You can view the inserted record on the console.

Similarly, use the `deleteContact(...)` and `updateContact(...)` methods to test the update and delete functionality.

Advantages

- This is an object-relational mapping technique used for accessing the databases. The domain objects are mapped to database entities.
- Preferable for simpler database schemas and tables with well-defined relationships.
- The developer don't have to deal with SQL. Realm-IO provides a higher level API for the create, read, update, and delete operations.

Limitations

- This technique is suitable for tables having well-defined relationships, and is not suitable for executing complex sub-queries and correlated sub-queries.
- Primary keys are not auto-generated in the current version.

Using the Shared Preferences Object

The following business scenario is implemented using the Shared Preferences Object class. This is an alternative solution for storing the both key and value data in Android.

Use Case Scenario:

1. Assuming your application requires key-value data storage.
2. You want to store data into an object and access it as needed.
3. You may not want to use the mobile database for storing data.
4. Design a main screen with "SPO" button.
5. Click on "SPO" button. User navigates to the next (user data) screen.
6. Design and create a user interface with user name, password, and cached input fields.
7. Add "Get Data" button.
8. Click on "Get Data" button to obtain the cached data.

The above described navigation scenario is shown in Figure 6-3.

Figure 6-3: Main and navigation screens

Tutorial 3: Saving and Reading Data using the Shared Preferences Object

The steps required to implement the above-specified business scenario using the Shared Preferences Object are listed below:

1. Create a layout file.
2. Create Activity classes
3. Test the application.

The above-specified steps are described in the following sections:

Step 1: Create a layout file

Here, reuse the previously created "activity_main.xml" file. Add the following button element to the layout file.

```
<Button
    android:id="@+id/spo_button"
    android:layout_width="200dp"
    android:layout_height="wrap_content"
    android:layout_marginBottom="5sp"
    android:layout_marginLeft="60dp"
    android:layout_marginRight="12dp"
    android:enabled="true"
    android:text="SPO"
    android:textSize="30sp"/>
```

Go to → res → layout → create "activity_spo.xml" file.

The following "activity_spo.xml" file is used to create the navigation (user data) screen. This screen reads the data stored in a Shared Preferences Object. This layout shows the user specific attributes such as user name, password, and so forth. The complete layout "activity_spo.xml" code is provided below.

```xml
<?xml version="1.0" encoding="utf-8"?>
<LinearLayout xmlns:android="http://schemas.android.com/apk/res/android"
    android:layout_width="fill_parent"
    android:layout_height="fill_parent"
    android:orientation="vertical"
    android:weightSum="1">

    <TextView
        android:layout_width="match_parent"
        android:layout_height="wrap_content"
        android:layout_marginTop="5dp"
        android:enabled="true"
        android:textColor="@color/material_blue_grey_950"
        android:text="User Name" />

    <EditText
        android:id="@+id/username"
        android:layout_width="match_parent"
        android:layout_height="wrap_content"
        android:enabled="false"
        android:textSize="30sp"/>

    <TextView
        android:layout_width="match_parent"
        android:layout_height="wrap_content"
        android:layout_marginTop="5dp"
        android:enabled="true"
        android:textColor="@color/material_blue_grey_950"
        android:text="Password:" />

    <EditText
        android:id="@+id/password"
        android:layout_width="match_parent"
        android:layout_height="wrap_content"
        android:enabled="false"
        android:textSize="30sp"/>

    <TextView
        android:layout_width="match_parent"
        android:layout_height="wrap_content"
        android:layout_marginTop="5dp"
        android:enabled="true"
        android:textColor="@color/material_blue_grey_950"
        android:text="Cached:" />

    <EditText
        android:id="@+id/cached"
        android:layout_width="match_parent"
        android:layout_height="wrap_content"
        android:enabled="false"
        android:textSize="30sp"/>
```

```
<Button
    android:id="@+id/get_data_button"
    android:layout_width="200dp"
    android:layout_height="wrap_content"
    android:layout_marginBottom="5sp"
    android:layout_marginLeft="12dp"
    android:layout_marginRight="12dp"
    android:enabled="true"
    android:text="Get Data"
    android:textSize="30sp" />

</LinearLayout>
```

Step 2: Create Activity classes

Here, reuse the `MainActivity.java` created in Tutorial -1. Add the following lines of code to the `onCreate()` method of `MainActivity.java` class.

```
Button spoButton = (Button) findViewById(R.id.spo_button);
spoButton.setEnabled(true);
spoButton.setOnClickListener(spoButtonListener);
```

The above code captures the "SPO" button click event. Add the following methods to `MainActivity.java` class to receive the button click event.

```
// Create an anonymous class to act as a button click listener
private View.OnClickListener spoButtonListener = new
View.OnClickListener() {
    public void onClick(View v) {
        showSPODataScreen();
    }
};

// Invoking the SPO activity
private void showSPODataScreen() {
    Intent intent = new Intent(this, SPOActivity.class);
    startActivity(intent);
}
```

The following `SPOActivity.java` class is used to create the user data screen with "GET DATA" button. This class renders the previously created "activity_spo.xml" file.

Listing 6-2 provides the SPO activity class. Note the code inline comments.

Listing 6-2: SPOActivity.java class.

```
package com.example.androidlearning.db;

import android.app.Activity;
import android.content.SharedPreferences;
import android.os.Bundle;
import android.preference.PreferenceManager;
import android.util.Log;
import android.view.View;
import android.widget.Button;
```

```java
import android.widget.EditText;

import com.example.androidlearning.R;

// SPOActivity.java
public class SPOActivity extends Activity {

    @Override
    protected void onCreate(Bundle savedInstanceState) {
        super.onCreate(savedInstanceState);
        setContentView(R.layout.activity_spo);

        // Creating shared preferences object to store data
        SharedPreferences preferences =
            PreferenceManager.getDefaultSharedPreferences(this);
        SharedPreferences.Editor editor = preferences.edit();

        // Adding data to shared preferences
        editor.putString("username", "Srinivas");
        editor.putString("password", "admin123");
        editor.putString("logged", "YES, I did");

        // Commiting the data
        editor.commit();

        Button getDataButton = (Button)
                findViewById(R.id.get_data_button);
        getDataButton.setEnabled(true);
        getDataButton.setOnClickListener(getDataButtonListener);
    }

    private View.OnClickListener getDataButtonListener = new
    View.OnClickListener() {
        public void onClick(View v) {
            callReadDataActivity();
        }
    };

    public void callReadDataActivity() {
        getSPOData();
    }

    private void getSPOData() {
        // Reading the saved data from shared preferences object
        SharedPreferences preferences =
            PreferenceManager.getDefaultSharedPreferences(this);
        String userName = preferences.getString("username", "NONE");
        String password = preferences.getString("password", "NONE");
        String logged = preferences.getString("logged", "NONE");

        // Setting the data to edit text fields
        EditText userNameEdit = (EditText) findViewById(R.id.username);
        userNameEdit.setText(userName);

        EditText passwordEdit = (EditText) findViewById(R.id.password);
        passwordEdit.setText(password);
```

```
        EditText cachedEdit = (EditText) findViewById(R.id.cached);
        cachedEdit.setText(logged);
    }
}
```

Step 3: Test the application.

Follow the below provided step-by-step instructions to test the application.

1. Start the emulator
2. Click on application Icon → Main screen will be displayed with "SPO" button
3. Click on "SPO" button
4. User data screen will be displayed (Refer to Figure 6-3)
5. Click on "GET DATA" button
6. The cached data will be displayed.

Advantages

- The shared preferences object is used for storing a preference's data both as key and value. Making it most suitable for storing simple data to be used as needed. This is similar to `java.util.Map` API.

Limitations

- Only suitable for storing simple data types.
- Most suitable for storing simple light-weight data with no entity relationships.
- The API is not designed for object-relational mapping or resultset to-object mapping.

File IO

Tutorial 4: Saving and Reading Data using JDK File IO

The following business scenario is implemented using the JDK file input-output API.

Use Case Scenario:

- Design a main screen with "File IO" button.
- Click on "File IO" button. User navigates to the next screen.
- Create a file and write data to the file
- Read the data from file and show it to user.

The above described navigation scenario is shown in Figure 6-4.

Figure 6-4: Main and navigation screens

The steps required to implement the above-specified business scenario using JDK File-IO API are listed below:

1. Create a layout file.
2. Create Activity classes
3. Test the application.

The above-specified steps are described in the following sections:

Step 1: Create a layout file

The following "activity_main.xml" file is used to create the main screen.

Here, reuse the previously created "activity_main.xml" file. Add the following button element to the layout file.

```
<Button
    android:id="@+id/flieio_button"
    android:layout_width="200dp"
    android:layout_height="wrap_content"
    android:layout_marginBottom="5sp"
    android:layout_marginLeft="60dp"
    android:layout_marginRight="12dp"
    android:enabled="true"
    android:text="SPO"
    android:textSize="30sp" />
```

The following "activity_fileio.xml" file is used to create the navigation (user data) screen. The complete "activity_fileio.xml" file code is provided below.

```
<RelativeLayout xmlns:android =
        "http://schemas.android.com/apk/res/android"
```

```
        xmlns:tools="http://schemas.android.com/tools"
        android:layout_width="match_parent"
        android:layout_height="match_parent"
        android:paddingLeft="@dimen/activity_horizontal_margin"
        android:paddingRight="@dimen/activity_horizontal_margin"
        android:paddingTop="@dimen/activity_vertical_margin"
        android:paddingBottom="@dimen/activity_vertical_margin" >

    <EditText
        android:id="@+id/ioname_edittext"
        android:layout_width="match_parent"
        android:layout_height="wrap_content"
        android:layout_marginTop="5dp"
        android:enabled="true"
        android:textSize="30sp" />

</RelativeLayout>
```

Step 2: Create Activity classes

Here, reuse the `MainActivity.java` created in Tutorial -1. Add the following lines of code to the `onCreate()` method of `MainActivity.java` class.

```
Button fileIOButton = (Button) findViewById(R.id.flieio_button);
fileIOButton.setEnabled(true);
fileIOButton.setOnClickListener(fileIOButtonListener);
```

The above code captures the "File IO" button click event. Add the following methods to `MainActivity.java` class to receive the button click event.

```
// Create an anonymous class to act as a button click listener
private View.OnClickListener spoButtonListener = new
View.OnClickListener() {
    public void onClick(View v) {
        createFile();
    }
};

// Invoking the File-IO activity
private void createFile() {
    Intent intent = new Intent(this, FileIOActivity.class);
    startActivity(intent);
}
```

The following `FileIOActivity.java` class is used to show the data to the user. This class renders the previously created layout "activity_fileio.xml" file.

Listing 6-3 provides the File-IO activity class. Note the code inline comments.

Listing 6-3: FileIOActivity.java class.

```
package com.example.androidlearning.db;

import android.app.Activity;
import android.content.Context;
```

```
import android.os.Bundle;
import android.util.Log;
import android.widget.EditText;

import com.example.androidlearning.R;

import java.io.BufferedReader;
import java.io.FileNotFoundException;
import java.io.IOException;
import java.io.InputStream;
import java.io.InputStreamReader;
import java.io.OutputStreamWriter;

// FileIOActivity.java
public class FileIOActivity extends Activity {

    @Override
    protected void onCreate(Bundle savedInstanceState) {
        super.onCreate(savedInstanceState);
        setContentView(R.layout.activity_fileio);

        // Writing data to a file
        writeToFile("Srinivas");

        // Reading data from a file
        String nameFromFile = readFromFile();
        EditText ioName =(EditText) findViewById(R.id.ioname_edittext);
        ioName.setText(nameFromFile);
    }

    private void writeToFile(String data) {
        try {
            OutputStreamWriter outputStreamWriter =
                new OutputStreamWriter(openFileOutput("config.txt",
                            Context.MODE_PRIVATE));
            outputStreamWriter.write(data);
            outputStreamWriter.close();
        } catch (IOException e) {
            Log.e("Exception", "File write failed: " + e.toString());
        }
    }

    private String readFromFile() {
        String data = "";
        try {
            InputStream inputStream = openFileInput("config.txt");
            if (inputStream != null) {
                InputStreamReader inputStreamReader = new
                        InputStreamReader(inputStream);
                BufferedReader bufferedReader = new
                        BufferedReader(inputStreamReader);
                String receiveString = "";
                StringBuilder stringBuilder = new StringBuilder();

                While ((receiveString = bufferedReader.readLine())
                        != null) {
                    stringBuilder.append(receiveString);
```

```
                }

                inputStream.close();
                data = stringBuilder.toString();
            }
        } catch (FileNotFoundException e) {
            Log.e("FileIOActivity", "File not found: " + e.toString());
        } catch (IOException e) {
            Log.e("FileIOActivity", "Can not read file: " +
                    e.toString());
        }

        return data;
    }
}
```

Step 3: Test the application.

Follow the below provided step-by-step instructions to test the application.

1. Start the emulator
2. Click on application Icon → Main screen will be displayed with "File IO" button
3. Click on "File IO" button
4. Data screen will be displayed (Refer to Figure 6-4)

Advantages

*   JDK's "java.io" package provides a simple and powerful API for system file input-output operations.
*   No additional software is needed; can use the JDK-provided "java.io" package API for File-IO operations. This is a very commonly used programming model in Java application development.
*   Simple to use, easy to implement, and commonly used Java programming model.

Limitations

*   Large files use a lot of memory.
*   Not suitable for performing create, read, update, or delete operations. JDK File-IO API is designed only for system file input-output operations, does not provide an SQL type programming model.
*   File-IO does not provide any inbuilt object-relational mapping programming model.

Comparison between SQLite and Ream IO

The following table summarizes the comparison between the various technical features of SQLite and Realm IO.

Ream IO	SQLite
This is an object-relational mapping technique used for accessing the databases. The domain objects are mapped to database entities.	SQL-based programming technique. Developer must map the resultset data to domain objects. Similar to JDBC-style programming model. Simple, flexible, easy to learn, smaller in package size, and provides powerful features for building SQL statements.
Preferable for simpler database schemas and tables that have well-defined relationships.	Uses the power of SQL statements. Developers can apply their SQL knowledge for database operations.
Separate codebase developed for the Android and iOS platforms.	Saves the data into a platform-independent file. Easy to port the database file from one platform to another.
Not packaged with Android platform. This an open-source framework developed for the Android platform.	Default database packaged with Android platform. No additional JAR's are required.
Provide support for Android and iOS platforms.	Developed for Android platform.
Primary keys are not auto-generated, will be available in future releases.	Primary keys are auto-generated.
POJO class must contain only getter and setter methods.	Can have non-getter and setter methods.

Summary

Figure 6-5 Mobile database persistence frameworks

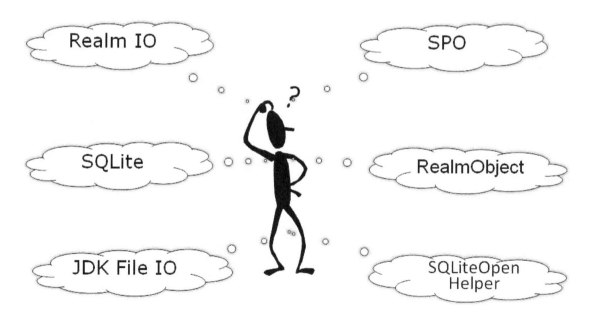

This section summarizes the mobile database frameworks provided features. Figure 6-5 summarizes the most important points described in this chapter.

- Realm IO is an object-relational mapping technique used to access databases. The domain objects are mapped to database entities.
- SQLite is an open-source light weight embedded mobile database. This is the default database provided with the Android platform.
- The JDK-provided "file-io" API can be used for reading and writing data streams in an Android application development.
- Android provides a `SharedPreferences` interface that can be used as a key-value data storage solution.

Chapter 7. Android Location Based Services

The very commonly used application in mobile devices is location based services (LBS). Google location play services API can be used to build the location-aware applications. This API provides visual representation of Google maps on mobile devices. For a given latitude and longitude; you can identify and pinpoint the location on a map.

This chapter will discuss the following topics:

* Add makers and titles to Google maps
* How to develop location-aware applications in Android.
* Using Google Maps API
* Introduction to Geocoding API

Google Maps API

Android provides `MapFragment` class which can be used to implement the location aware applications. An example use of "gms" map fragment is provided below.

```
<fragment
    xmlns:android="http://schemas.android.com/apk/res/android"
    android:id="@+id/map"
    android:layout_width="match_parent"
    android:layout_height="match_parent"
    class="com.google.android.gms.maps.MapFragment"/>
```

The following code obtains the map fragment object.

```
MapFragment mapFragment = (MapFragment)
            getFragmentManager().findFragmentById(R.id.map);
map = mapFragment.getMap();
```

The following code pinpoint the location on a map for a given latitude and longitude.

```
LatLng pinLocation = new LatLng(latitude, longitude);
map.addMarker(new MarkerOptions().position(pinLocation));
```

The following code enables the building view on a map.

```
map.setBuildingsEnabled(true);
```

Similarly, the following code enables the traffic view on a map.

```
map.setTrafficEnabled(true);
```

The following code enable the current location.

```
map.setMyLocationEnabled(true);
```

Geocoder API

The geocoder API is used for handling geocoding and reverse geocoding. The geocoding is the process of transforming street address or other textual data into a latitude and longitude. The reverse geocoding is the process of transforming latitude and longitude into a location address.

The following code obtains the location address from a given latitude and longitude.

```
Geocoder geocoder = new Geocoder(this, Locale.getDefault());
List<android.location.Address> addresses =
        geocoder.getFromLocation(latitude, longitude, 1);
```

The following code obtains the address details such as city, state, county, and so forth.

```
String address = addresses.get(0).getAddressLine(0);
String city = addresses.get(0).getLocality();
String state = addresses.get(0).getAdminArea();
String country = addresses.get(0).getCountryName();
String zipCode = addresses.get(0).getPostalCode();
String knownName = addresses.get(0).getFeatureName();
```

Tutorial: Pinpoint the Locations on Google Map

Figure 7-1: Showing location on Google maps

Use Case Scenario:

The following business scenario is implemented using Google LBS API.

- Pinpoint the location on google maps for a given latitude and longitude.
- Specify the title for a location
- Show the address on a map

The above described scenario is shown in Figure 7-1.

The steps required to implement the above-specified scenario using Google maps API are listed below:

1. Get the your SHA-1 fingerprint certificate
2. Register with Google developer console
3. Obtain the Google maps API key for your application from Google developer console
4. Install Google play services
5. Work on your configurations
6. Connect your Android device
7. Run your application

The above-specified steps are described in the following sections:

Step 1: Get your SHA-1 Certificate Fingerprint

This SHA1 finger print is required to obtain the maps API key from Google developer console.

1. Go to your JDK bin directory → C:\jdk1.7.0\bin>

Figure 7-2: SHA1 certificate fingerprint on command line

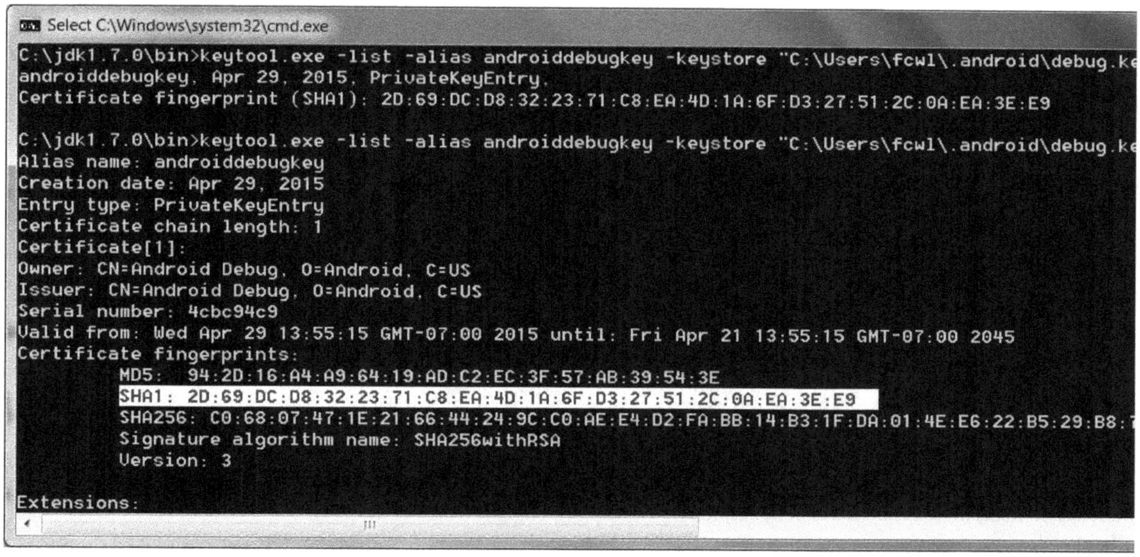

2. Execute the following JDK keytool command with the following options.

```
keytool.exe -list -alias androiddebugkey -keystore
"C:\Users\xxxxx\.android\debug.keystore" -storepass android -keypass
android -v
```

xxxxx = your user name – For Windows, this will be inside the "Users" directory.

3. Obtain the SHA1 certificate fingerprint from the command window. Refer to Figure 7-2 for details.

Step 2: Register with Google Developer Console

1. Open Google developer console from your browser

https://console.developers.google.com/project

2. Select an existing project or create a new project. Refer to Figure 7-3

Figure 7-3: Google developer console

3. Select Google Maps API and create an API key. Obtain your API key from Google developer console. Refer to Figure 7-4.

Figure 7-4: Google developer console – create your API key

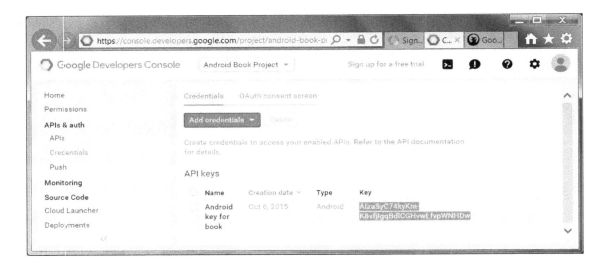

Enter "package name" and your "SHA1 certificate fingerprint" to create an API key.

Get the package name from application manifest file. An example package name is provided below

```
<manifest xmlns:android="http://schemas.android.com/apk/res/android"
    package="com.example.andriodlearning" >
    ...
</manifest>
```

Step 3: Obtain the Google Maps API Key for Your Application

Get your Google maps API key from Google developer console (Refer to Figure 7.4). The generated key for my application is provided below. Don't use this key in your application. Generate your own key.

AlzaSyC74kyKm-K8vfjIgqBdlCGHvwLfvpWNHDw

Step 4: Install Google Play Services.

Open SDK Manager in your Android studio → Go to extras → Install Google play services. Refer to Figure 7-5.

Figure 7-5: Installing google play services

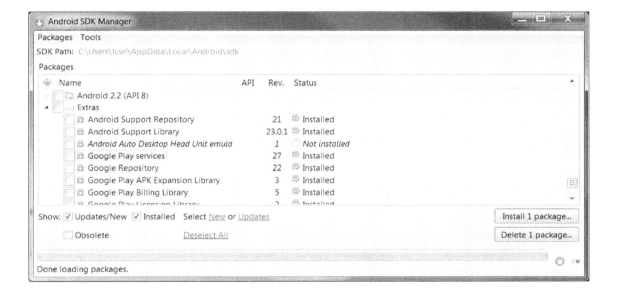

Step 5: Work on Your Configurations

Add permissions to your project. Add the following permissions to your application manifest file.

```
<uses-permission android:name="android.permission.INTERNET" />
<uses-permission android:name=
        "android.permission.WRITE_EXTERNAL_STORAGE" />
<uses-permission android:name="android.permission.ACCESS_WIFI_STATE" />
<uses-permission android:name="android.permission.CHANGE_WIFI_STATE" />
<uses-permission android:name="android.permission.CHANGE_NETWORK_STATE"/>
<uses-permission android:name="android.permission.ACCESS_NETWORK_STATE"/>
<uses-permission android:name=
```

```
                    "android.permission.ACCESS_COARSE_LOCATION"/>
<uses-permission android:name="android.permission.ACCESS_FINE_LOCATION"/>
```

Add the following "uses feature" element to your application manifest file.

```
<uses-feature
    android:glEsVersion="0x00020000"
    android:required="true"/>
```

Add the following "metadata" elements to your application manifest file. Here, make sure you are using the correct API key.

```
<meta-data
    android:name="com.google.android.geo.API_KEY"
    android:value="AIzaSyC74kyKm-K8vfjIgqBdlCGHvwLfvpWNHDw"/>

<meta-data
    android:name="com.google.android.gms.version"
    android:value="7571000"/>
```

Add the following dependencies to your application "build.gradle" file.

```
compile 'com.google.android.gms:play-services:7.5.0'
compile 'com.google.android.gms:play-services-maps:7.5.0'
```

Step 6: Create your Main Activity Layout File

Go to res → layout → create "activity_main.xml" file

The following "activity_main.xml" file is used to create the main screen.

```
<RelativeLayout xmlns:android =
    "http://schemas.android.com/apk/res/android"
    xmlns:tools="http://schemas.android.com/tools"
    android:layout_width="match_parent"
    android:layout_height="match_parent"
    android:paddingLeft="@dimen/activity_horizontal_margin"
    android:paddingRight="@dimen/activity_horizontal_margin"
    android:paddingTop="@dimen/activity_vertical_margin"
    android:paddingBottom="@dimen/activity_vertical_margin"
    tools:context=".MainActivity">

    <LinearLayout
        android:layout_width="match_parent"
        android:layout_height="wrap_content"
        android:layout_gravity="center_horizontal"
        android:orientation="vertical">

        <Button
            android:id="@+id/maps_button"
            android:layout_width="250dp"
            android:layout_height="wrap_content"
            android:layout_marginBottom="5sp"
            android:layout_marginLeft="60dp"
            android:layout_marginRight="12dp"
```

```
                    android:enabled="true"
                    android:text="Show Map"
                    android:textSize="30sp"/>

        </LinearLayout>
</RelativeLayout>
```

Step 7: Create Your Maps Activity Layout File

Go to res → layout → create "activity_lbs.xml" file. The following "activity_lbs.xml" file is used to add the map fragment.

```xml
<?xml version="1.0" encoding="utf-8"?>
<fragment
    xmlns:android="http://schemas.android.com/apk/res/android"
    android:id="@+id/map"
    android:layout_width="match_parent"
    android:layout_height="match_parent"
    class="com.google.android.gms.maps.MapFragment"/>
```

Step 8: Create Main Activity Class

The following `MainActivity.java` class is used to create the main screen with "Show Map" button. This class renders the previously created layout "activity_main.xml" file.

Listing 7-1 provides the main activity class. Note the code inline comments.

Listing 7-1: MainActivity.java class.

```java
package com.example.androidlearning;

import android.app.Activity;
import android.content.Intent;
import android.os.Bundle;
import android.view.View;
import android.widget.Button;

import com.example.androidlearning.lbs.MapsActivity;

// MainActivity.java
public class MainActivity extends Activity {

    @Override
    protected void onCreate(Bundle savedInstanceState) {
        super.onCreate(savedInstanceState);
        setContentView(R.layout.activity_main);

        // Button event listener to capture the click event
        Button mapsButton = (Button) findViewById(R.id.maps_button);
        mapsButton.setEnabled(true);
        mapsButton.setOnClickListener(mapsButtonListener);
    }

    // Create an anonymous class to act as a button click listener
    private View.OnClickListener mapsButtonListener = new
        View.OnClickListener() {
```

```
        public void onClick(View v) {
            callMapsActivity();
        }
    };

    // Calling maps activity class
    private void callMapsActivity() {
        Intent intent = new Intent(this, MapsActivity.class);
        startActivity(intent);
    }
}
```

Step 9: Create the Required Domain Object Classes

The `Geometry` domain object class code is provided below.

```
package com.example.androidlearning.lbs;

public class Geometry {

    private double latitude;
    private double longitude;
    private String title;
    private String address;

    ...

    // Add getter and setters
}
```

Step 10: Create Maps Activity Class

The following `MapsActivity.java` class is used to display the Google map screen. This class renders the previously created "activity_lbs.xml" file.

Listing 7-2 provides the Maps activity class. Note the code inline comments.

Listing 7-2: MapActivity.java class.

```
package com.example.androidlearning.lbs;
import android.os.Bundle;
import android.support.v4.app.FragmentActivity;
import android.util.Log;

import com.example.androidlearning.R;
import com.example.androidlearning.spring.ProxyAuthenticator;
import com.google.android.gms.maps.GoogleMap;
import com.google.android.gms.maps.MapFragment;
import com.google.android.gms.maps.model.BitmapDescriptorFactory;
import com.google.android.gms.maps.model.LatLng;
import com.google.android.gms.maps.model.MarkerOptions;

import java.net.Authenticator;
import java.util.ArrayList;
import java.util.List;
```

```java
// MapsActivity.java
public class MapsActivity extends FragmentActivity {

    GoogleMap map;

    @Override
    protected void onCreate(Bundle savedInstanceState) {
        super.onCreate(savedInstanceState);

        setContentView(R.layout.activity_lbs);

        // Pinpoint the locations on a map
        setupMapIfRequired();
    }

    // Show map on screen
    private void setupMapIfRequired() {
        if(map == null) {
            MapFragment mapFragment = (MapFragment)
                getFragmentManager().findFragmentById(R.id.map);
            map = mapFragment.getMap();

            if(map != null) {
                map.setMyLocationEnabled(true);
                showLatLongOnGoogleMap();
            }
        }
    }

    // Show locations on a map
    private void showLatLongOnGoogleMap() {
        // List of geometry objects with latitude and longitude
        List<Geometry> dataList = new ArrayList<Geometry>();
        Geometry geometry = new Geometry();
        geometry.setLatitude(47.6097);
        geometry.setLongitude(-122.3331);
        geometry.setTitle("Seatle_1");
        geometry.setAddress("3718 Rosedale St NW, Gig Harbor, WA");
        dataList.add(geometry);

        geometry = new Geometry();
        geometry.setLatitude(45.6097);
        geometry.setLongitude(-120.3331);
        geometry.setTitle("Seatle_2");
        geometry.setAddress("735 12th St SE Auburn, WA");
        dataList.add(geometry);

        geometry = new Geometry();
        geometry.setLatitude(46.6097);
        geometry.setLongitude( -121.3331);
        geometry.setTitle("Seatle_3");
        geometry.setAddress("Vashon Island, WA");
        dataList.add(geometry);

        // Looping through data to show locations on map
        for (int i = 0; i < dataList.size(); i++) {
```

```
            double latitude = dataList.get(i).getLatitude();
            double longitude =  dataList.get(i).getLongitude();

            LatLng pinLocation = new LatLng(latitude, longitude);
            map.addMarker(new MarkerOptions().
                position(pinLocation).
                title(dataList.get(i).getTitle()).
                snippet(dataList.get(i).getAddress()).
                icon(BitmapDescriptorFactory.
                defaultMarker(BitmapDescriptorFactory.HUE_GREEN)));

            // Enabling buildings view
            map.setBuildingsEnabled(true);
        }
    }
}
```

Step 11: Connect Your Android Device and Test Your Application to View the Map

Follow the below provided step-by-step instructions to test the application.

1. Use your mobile device to view the map.
2. Connect your mobile device
3. Run the application on your device
4. Main screen will be shown with "Show Map" button.
5. Click on "Show Map" button.
6. Location markers will be shown on a map. Refer to Figure 7-6.

Figure 7-6: Location markers on Google maps

Chapter 8. Practice Project

This chapter will help you to develop a practice project. This will help you to bring up to the speed and provides more practice on coding. This project is about student learning management system using material navigation drawer. The following widgets are used while developing this project.

- Material Drawer
- Recycler View
- Material themes and colors
- Menus and menu icons
- Material toolbar
- Activities, intents, and fragments

Material Drawer

The material navigation drawer is a most commonly found pattern in Google applications which slides from left to right with a toggled hamburger icon on the tool bar. A material drawer is used for navigating to various pages in your application. You can build your own material drawer using Material tool bar, cards and recycler views. The following practice project will help you to develop a student learning management system using material navigation drawer.

Project Tutorial: Develop a Practice Project

Implement the following business scenario using material navigation drawer.

Use Case Scenario:

- Develop an application specific toolbar with material colors. (Refer to Figure 8-1)
- Develop a material navigation drawer with Home, Classes, Assignments, Tests, Grades, and Notifications menu icons.
- Click and hamburger icon (Refer to Figure 8-1)
- Opens a navigation drawer which slides from left to right.
- Click on Home → Home page will be displayed
- Click on Classes → Classes page will be displayed
- Click on Assignments → Assignments page will be displayed
- Click on Tests → Tests page will be displayed
- Click on Grades → Grades page will be displayed
- Click on Notifications → Notifications page will be displayed
- Click on menu → menu will be displayed with items

The above described scenario is shown in Figure 8-1.

Figure 8-1: Navigation material drawer with material toolbar.

The steps required to implement the above-specified scenario are listed below:

1. Design a window and choose the required material colors for your application
2. Create a new project
3. Add required titles and static labels
4. Specify navigation drawer width
5. Create a new material theme
6. Apply the new material theme
7. Run the application.
8. Add a toolbar.
9. Include toolbar in your main layout file.
10. Run the application.
11. Add menu, icons, and toolbar title
12. Run the application.
13. Add navigation drawer dependencies
14. Create required model classes
15. Navigation drawer items
16. Create RecyclerView Adapter class
17. Create a Fragment to inflate the navigation drawer
18. Adding drawer layout widget to your main layout
19. Create one fragment for each menu click item.
20. Update main activity class to display fragment body
21. Check your project structure in Android studio
22. Test the application
23. Add a new menu with menu items to the toolbar menu
24. Test the application

The above-specified steps are described in the following sections:

Step 1: Design a Window and Choose the Required Material Colors

Choose material colors for your window, toolbar, and application status bar. Figure 8-2 shows the design of your main screen.

Figure 8-2: Navigation material drawer with material colors.

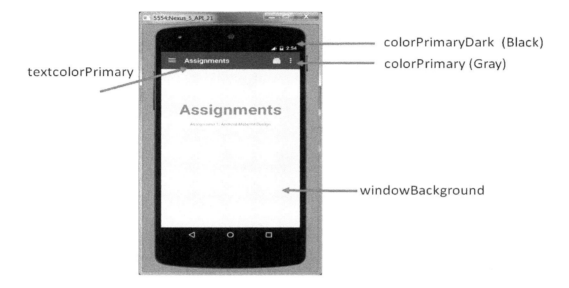

Figure 8-3: New project window in Android studio.

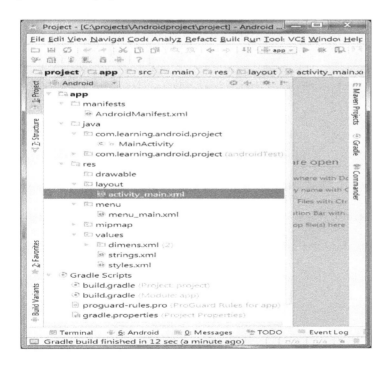

Step 2: Create a New Project

Create a new project with required details in Android studio. Choose a blank activity. The structure of the new project is shown in Figure 8-3.

Step 3: Add Required Titles and Static Labels

Go to → res → values → Open "string.xml" file.

This file is available in "values" directory. This file is used to add titles, labels, and any other required static values. Update "strings.xml" with the following values.

```xml
<resources>
    <string name="app_name">Material Drawer</string>

    <string name="action_settings">Settings</string>
    <string name="action_search">Search</string>
    <string name="drawer_open">Open</string>
    <string name="drawer_close">Close</string>

    <string name="nav_item_home">Home</string>
    <string name="nav_item_classes">Classes</string>
    <string name="nav_item_assignments">Assignments</string>
    <string name="nav_item_tests">Tests</string>
    <string name="nav_item_grades">Grades</string>
    <string name="nav_item_notifications">Notifications</string>

    <!-- navigation drawer item labels  -->
    <string-array name="nav_drawer_labels">
        <item>@string/nav_item_home</item>
        <item>@string/nav_item_classes</item>
        <item>@string/nav_item_assignments</item>
        <item>@string/nav_item_tests</item>
        <item>@string/nav_item_grades</item>
        <item>@string/nav_item_notifications</item>
    </string-array>

</resources>
```

Step 4: Specify Navigation Drawer Width

Go to → res → values → Open "dimens.xml" file.

This file is available in "values" directory. Add the navigation drawer width element to the existing XML file.

```xml
<resources>
    <!-- Default screen margins, per the Android Design guidelines. -->
    <dimen name="activity_horizontal_margin">16dp</dimen>
    <dimen name="activity_vertical_margin">16dp</dimen>

    <dimen name="nav_drawer_width">260dp</dimen>
</resources>
```

Step 5: Create a New Material Theme

Go to → res → values → Open "styles.xml" file.

This file is available in "values" directory. Add a new custom theme for your application. The minimum required API level for material design is 21. Update "build.gradle" with minSdkVersion = 21.

Theme name → MyMaterialTheme

Theme colors → material_grey_800, primary_dark_material_dark, and material_grey_600.

Refer to the below provided "styles.xml" file for details.

```
<resources>

    <!-- Base application theme. -->
    <style name="AppTheme" parent="Theme.AppCompat.Light.DarkActionBar">
        <!-- Customize your theme here. -->
    </style>

    <style name="MyMaterialTheme" parent="GrayMaterialTheme.Base">
        <item name="android:windowContentTransitions">true</item>
        <item name="android:windowAllowEnterTransitionOverlap">true
        </item>
        <item name="android:windowAllowReturnTransitionOverlap">true
        </item>
        <item name="android:windowSharedElementEnterTransition">
            @android:transition/move</item>
        <item name="android:windowSharedElementExitTransition">
            @android:transition/move</item>
    </style>

    <style name="GrayMaterialTheme.Base"
        parent="Theme.AppCompat.Light.DarkActionBar">
        <item name="windowNoTitle">true</item>
        <item name="windowActionBar">false</item>
        <item name="colorPrimary">@color/material_grey_800</item>
        <item name="colorPrimaryDark">
            @color/primary_dark_material_dark
        </item>
        <item name="colorAccent">@color/material_grey_600</item>
    </style>

</resources>
```

Step 6: Apply the New Material Theme

Go to → manifests → Open "ApplicationManifest.xml" file.

Apply the theme. Update the "android:theme" attribute.

```
android:theme="@style/MyMaterialTheme"
```

The complete application manifest file is provided below.

```xml
<?xml version="1.0" encoding="utf-8"?>
<manifest xmlns:android="http://schemas.android.com/apk/res/android"
        package="com.learning.android.project" >

    <application
        android:allowBackup="true"
        android:icon="@mipmap/ic_launcher"
        android:label="@string/app_name"
        android:theme="@style/MyMaterialTheme">

        <activity
            android:name=".MainActivity"
            android:label="@string/app_name" >
            <intent-filter>
                <action android:name="android.intent.action.MAIN"/>

                <category
                    android:name="android.intent.category.LAUNCHER"/>
            </intent-filter>
        </activity>
    </application>
</manifest>
```

Step 7: Run the Application.

Run the application. See the black application notification bar as shown in Figure 8-4.

Figure 8-4: Application screen with application bar

Step 8: Add a Toolbar.

Go to → res → layout → create "toolbar.xml" file.

Add a toolbar to your application. Add the `Toolbar` widget to "toolbar.xml" file. The complete "toolbar.xml" file is provided below.

```xml
<?xml version="1.0" encoding="utf-8"?>
<android.support.v7.widget.Toolbar
xmlns:android="http://schemas.android.com/apk/res/android"
    xmlns:local="http://schemas.android.com/apk/res-auto"
    android:id="@+id/toolbar"
    android:layout_width="match_parent"
    android:layout_height="wrap_content"
    android:background="?attr/colorPrimary"
    android:minHeight="?attr/actionBarSize"
    local:popupTheme="@style/ThemeOverlay.AppCompat.Light"
    local:theme="@style/ThemeOverlay.AppCompat.Dark.ActionBar"/>
```

Step 9: Include Toolbar in Your Main Layout File.

Go to → res → layout → open "activity_main.xml" file.

Include the previously created toolbar layout in your main layout file. The complete layout "activity_main.xml" file is provided below.

```xml
<RelativeLayout xmlns:android=
    "http://schemas.android.com/apk/res/android"
    xmlns:tools="http://schemas.android.com/tools"
    android:layout_width="match_parent"
    android:layout_height="match_parent"
    android:paddingLeft="@dimen/activity_horizontal_margin"
    android:paddingRight="@dimen/activity_horizontal_margin"
    android:paddingTop="@dimen/activity_vertical_margin"
    android:paddingBottom="@dimen/activity_vertical_margin"
    tools:context=".MainActivity">

    <LinearLayout
        android:layout_width="fill_parent"
        android:layout_height="wrap_content"
        android:layout_alignParentTop="true"
        android:orientation="vertical">

        <include
            android:id="@+id/toolbar"
            layout="@layout/toolbar" />

    </LinearLayout>

</RelativeLayout>
```

Step 10: Run the Application.

Run the application. You can view the application with toolbar without titles and menu as shown in Figure 8-5.

Figure 8-5: Application screen with material toolbar

Step 11: Add Menu, Icons, and Toolbar Title

Download search icon (search.png) from internet. Copy the "search.png" icon into "drawable" directory.

Add search icon to your toolbar menu. Open "menu_main.xml". This file is available in "menu" directory.

Open → menu → menu_main.xml. The complete "menu_main.xml" file is provided below.

```
<menu xmlns:android="http://schemas.android.com/apk/res/android"
    xmlns:app="http://schemas.android.com/apk/res-auto"
    xmlns:tools="http://schemas.android.com/tools"
    tools:context=".MainActivity">

    <item
        android:id="@+id/action_settings"
        android:orderInCategory="100"
        android:title="@string/action_settings"
        app:showAsAction="never" />

    <item
        android:id="@+id/action_search"
```

```
                    android:title="@string/action_search"
                    android:orderInCategory="100"
                  . android:icon="@drawable/search"
                    app:showAsAction="ifRoom" />

</menu>
```

Add menu to the toolbar. Your activity must extend the `AppCompatActivity` class. An example code is provided below.

```
public class MainActivity extends AppCompatActivity {
    ...
}
```

Enable the toolbar. Open `MainActivity.java` class. The `setSupportActionBar()` method adds the toolbar to your application. Update `onCreate()` method of your main activity class. An example code is provided below.

```
Toolbar toolbar = (Toolbar) findViewById(R.id.toolbar);
setSupportActionBar(toolbar);
getSupportActionBar().setDisplayShowHomeEnabled(true);
```

The complete `MainActivity.java` class code is provided below.

```
package com.learning.android.project;

import android.support.v7.app.ActionBarActivity;
import android.os.Bundle;
import android.support.v7.app.AppCompatActivity;
import android.support.v7.widget.Toolbar;
import android.view.Menu;
import android.view.MenuItem;

// MainActivity.java
public class MainActivity extends AppCompatActivity {

    @Override
    protected void onCreate(Bundle savedInstanceState) {
        super.onCreate(savedInstanceState);
        setContentView(R.layout.activity_main);

        // Adding tool bar
        Toolbar toolbar = (Toolbar) findViewById(R.id.toolbar);
        setSupportActionBar(toolbar);
        getSupportActionBar().setDisplayShowHomeEnabled(true);
    }

    @Override
    public boolean onCreateOptionsMenu(Menu menu) {
        /* Inflate the menu; this adds items to the
            action bar if it is present. */
        getMenuInflater().inflate(R.menu.menu_main, menu);
        return true;
    }
```

```
@Override
public boolean onOptionsItemSelected(MenuItem item) {
    // Handle action bar item clicks here. The action bar will
    // automatically handle clicks on the Home/Up button, so long
    // as you specify a parent activity in AndroidManifest.xml.
    int id = item.getItemId();

    //noinspection SimplifiableIfStatement
    if (id == R.id.action_settings) {
        return true;
    }

    return super.onOptionsItemSelected(item);
}
}
```

Step 12: Run the Application.

Run the application. You can view the application toolbar with menu, search icon, and title as shown in Figure 8-6.

Figure 8-6: Application screen with material toolbar and menu

Step 13: Add Navigation Drawer Dependencies

The material navigation drawer is a most commonly found pattern in Google applications which slides from left to right with a toggled hamburger icon on the tool bar. A material drawer is used for navigating to various pages in your application. You can build your own material drawer using Material tool bar, cards and recycler views.

Add cards and recycler view dependencies to your application manifest file. An example code is provided below.

```
dependencies {
    compile fileTree(dir: 'libs', include: ['*.jar'])
    compile 'com.android.support:appcompat-v7:23.0.1'
    compile 'com.android.support:recyclerview-v7:22.2.+'
}
```

Step 14: Create Required Model Classes

Create a model class `DrawerDVO.java`. This class is used to store data.

```
package com.learning.android.materialdrawer;

public class DrawerDVO {

    private String title;

    public DrawerDVO(){
    }

    public String getTitle() {
        return title;
    }

    public void setTitle(String title) {
        this.title = title;
    }
}
```

Step 15: Navigation Drawer Items

Go to res → layout → create drawer_row.xml" file. This layout file renders the each item of a navigation drawer.

```
<?xml version="1.0" encoding="utf-8"?>
<RelativeLayout xmlns:android=
    "http://schemas.android.com/apk/res/android"
    android:layout_width="match_parent"
    android:layout_height="wrap_content"
    android:clickable="true">

    <TextView
        android:id="@+id/title"
        android:layout_width="fill_parent"
        android:layout_height="wrap_content"
        android:paddingLeft="30dp"
        android:paddingTop="10dp"
        android:paddingBottom="10dp"
        android:textSize="15dp"
        android:textStyle="bold"/>
```

```
</RelativeLayout>
```

Now create navigation drawer layout. This layout renders the navigation drawer which slides from left to right.

You can add an image to the navigation drawer header. The following code adds an image to the header.

Go to res → drawable → Add "my_image.jpg"

```
<ImageView
        android:layout_width="70dp"
        android:layout_height="70dp"
        android:src="@drawable/my_image"
        android:scaleType="fitCenter"
        android:layout_centerInParent="true"/>
```

Add the `RecyclerView` widget to your navigation drawer. A `RecyclerView` widget is a pluggable version of the list view. This widget is used for displaying the data lists. Recycler view renders the items inside your drawer. An example use of this widget is provided below.

```
<android.support.v7.widget.RecyclerView>
```

Go to res → layout → Create "navigation_drawer.xml" layout file. The complete layout XML file is provided below.

```
<RelativeLayout xmlns:android=
"http://schemas.android.com/apk/res/android"
     android:layout_width="match_parent"
     android:layout_height="match_parent"
     android:background="@android:color/white">


    <RelativeLayout
        android:id="@+id/nav_header_container"
        android:layout_width="match_parent"
        android:layout_height="140dp"
        android:layout_alignParentTop="true"
        android:background="@color/material_grey_800">

        <ImageView
            android:layout_width="70dp"
            android:layout_height="70dp"
            android:src="@drawable/my_image"
            android:scaleType="fitCenter"
            android:layout_centerInParent="true" />

    </RelativeLayout>


    <android.support.v7.widget.RecyclerView
        android:id="@+id/drawerList"
        android:layout_width="match_parent"
        android:layout_height="wrap_content"
        android:layout_below="@id/nav_header_container"
```

```
                  android:layout_marginTop="15dp" />

</RelativeLayout>
```

Step 16: Create RecyclerView Adapter Class

The Adapter class must extend the `RecyclerView.Adapter` class. This adapter class is an intermediate class between recycler view and dataset. Adapter class obtains the data from dataset; and pass it to the UI layout manger to display it on the screen.

This adapter class must override the `onBindViewHolder(...)` and `onCreateViewHolder(...)` methods. The complete adapter class code is provided below.

The following adapter class inflates the "drawer_row.xml" file; and renders the data for each item inside the drawer. Sets the each item value to "title" text field.

```java
package com.learning.android.project;

import android.content.Context;
import android.support.v7.widget.RecyclerView;
import android.view.LayoutInflater;
import android.view.View;
import android.view.ViewGroup;
import android.widget.TextView;

import java.util.Collections;
import java.util.List;

// DrawerAdapter.java
public class DrawerAdapter extends
        RecyclerView.Adapter<DrawerAdapter.MyViewHolder> {

    List<DrawerDVO> data = new ArrayList<>();
    private LayoutInflater inflater;
    private Context context;

    // Adapter constructor - Initialize the data
    public DrawerAdapter(Context context, List<DrawerDVO> data) {
        this.context = context;
        inflater = LayoutInflater.from(context);
        this.data = data;
    }

    @Override
    // Inflating the layout file
    public MyViewHolder onCreateViewHolder(ViewGroup parent,
        int viewType) {
        View view = inflater.inflate(
                R.layout.drawer_row, parent, false);
        MyViewHolder holder = new MyViewHolder(view);
        return holder;
    }

    @Override
    // Setting the item data
```

```
public void onBindViewHolder(MyViewHolder holder, int position) {
    DrawerDVO current = data.get(position);
    holder.title.setText(current.getTitle());
}

@Override
public int getItemCount() {
    return data.size();
}

// Obtains the item view
public class MyViewHolder extends RecyclerView.ViewHolder {
    TextView title;
    public MyViewHolder(View itemView) {
        super(itemView);
        title = (TextView) itemView.findViewById(R.id.title);
    }
}
}
```

Step 17: Create a Fragment to Inflate the Navigation Drawer

Create a `DrawerFragment.java` class. This class inflates the "navigation_drawer.xml" layout. This class uses recycler view adapter to obtain the data items and renders in a drawer layout.

```
package com.learning.android.project;

import android.content.Context;
import android.os.Bundle;
import android.support.v4.app.Fragment;
import android.support.v4.widget.DrawerLayout;
import android.support.v7.app.ActionBarDrawerToggle;
import android.support.v7.widget.LinearLayoutManager;
import android.support.v7.widget.RecyclerView;
import android.support.v7.widget.Toolbar;
import android.view.GestureDetector;
import android.view.LayoutInflater;
import android.view.MotionEvent;
import android.view.View;
import android.view.ViewGroup;

import java.util.ArrayList;
import java.util.List;

// DrawerFragment.java
public class DrawerFragment extends Fragment {

    private DrawerLayout drawerLayout;
    private View containerView;
    private static String[] titles = null;
    private FragmentDrawerListener drawerListener;

    public void setDrawerListener(FragmentDrawerListener listener) {
        this.drawerListener = listener;
    }
```

```java
public interface FragmentDrawerListener {
    public void onDrawerItemSelected(View view, int position);
}

public static List<DrawerDVO> getData() {
    List<DrawerDVO> data = new ArrayList<>();

    // Preparing navigation drawer items
    for (int i = 0; i < titles.length; i++) {
        DrawerDVO navItem = new DrawerDVO();
        navItem.setTitle(titles[i]);
        data.add(navItem);
    }
    return data;
}

@Override
public void onCreate(Bundle savedInstanceState) {
    super.onCreate(savedInstanceState);

    // nav_drawer_labels labels from strings.xml property file
    this.titles = getActivity().getResources().
        getStringArray(R.array.nav_drawer_labels);
}

@Override
public View onCreateView(LayoutInflater inflater,
        ViewGroup container, Bundle savedInstanceState) {

    // Inflating view layout
    View layout = inflater.inflate(R.layout.navigation_drawer,
                        container, false);
    RecyclerView recyclerView = (RecyclerView)
                    layout.findViewById(R.id.drawerList);

    DrawerAdapter adapter = new DrawerAdapter(getActivity(),
                        getData());
    recyclerView.setAdapter(adapter);
    recyclerView.setLayoutManager(new
                LinearLayoutManager(getActivity()));
    recyclerView.addOnItemTouchListener(new RecyclerTouchListener(
            getActivity(), recyclerView, new ClickListener() {
        @Override
        public void onClick(View view, int position) {
            drawerListener.onDrawerItemSelected(view, position);
            drawerLayout.closeDrawer(containerView);
        }

        @Override
        public void onLongClick(View view, int position) {
        }
    }));

    return layout;
}
```

```java
public void setUp(int fragmentId, DrawerLayout drawerLayout,
        final Toolbar toolbar) {
    containerView = getActivity().findViewById(fragmentId);
    drawerLayout = drawerLayout;
    final ActionBarDrawerToggle mDrawerToggle =
        new ActionBarDrawerToggle(getActivity(), drawerLayout,
        toolbar, R.string.drawer_open, R.string.drawer_close) {
        @Override
        public void onDrawerOpened(View drawerView) {
            super.onDrawerOpened(drawerView);
            getActivity().invalidateOptionsMenu();
        }

        @Override
        public void onDrawerClosed(View drawerView) {
            super.onDrawerClosed(drawerView);
            getActivity().invalidateOptionsMenu();
        }

        @Override
        public void onDrawerSlide(View drawerView,
                float slideOffset) {
            super.onDrawerSlide(drawerView, slideOffset);
            toolbar.setAlpha(1 - slideOffset / 2);
        }
    };

    drawerLayout.setDrawerListener(mDrawerToggle);
    drawerLayout.post(new Runnable() {
        @Override
        public void run() {
            mDrawerToggle.syncState();
        }
    });
}

public static interface ClickListener {
    public void onClick(View view, int position);
    public void onLongClick(View view, int position);
}

public static class RecyclerTouchListener implements
                    RecyclerView.OnItemTouchListener {
    private GestureDetector gestureDetector;
    private ClickListener clickListener;

    public RecyclerTouchListener(Context context,
            final RecyclerView recyclerView,
            final ClickListener clickListener) {
        this.clickListener = clickListener;
        gestureDetector = new GestureDetector(context,
            new GestureDetector.SimpleOnGestureListener() {
            @Override
            public boolean onSingleTapUp(MotionEvent e) {
                return true;
            }
```

```
                @Override
                public void onLongPress(MotionEvent e) {
                    View child = recyclerView.findChildViewUnder(
                                    e.getX(), e.getY());
                    if (child != null && clickListener != null) {
                        clickListener.onLongClick(child,
                                recyclerView.getChildPosition(child));
                    }
                }
            });
        }

        @Override
        public boolean onInterceptTouchEvent(RecyclerView rv,
                        MotionEvent e) {
            View child = rv.findChildViewUnder(e.getX(), e.getY());
            if (child != null && clickListener != null &&
                gestureDetector.onTouchEvent(e)) {
                clickListener.onClick(child,
                            rv.getChildPosition(child));
            }
            return false;
        }

        @Override
        public void onTouchEvent(RecyclerView rv, MotionEvent e) {
        }

        @Override
        public void onRequestDisallowInterceptTouchEvent(boolean
                disallowIntercept) {
        }
    }
}
```

Step 18: Adding Drawer Layout Widget to Your Main Layout

Open "activity_main.xml" layout file. Add drawer layout widget to the "activity_main.xml" file. This widget display the navigation drawer with menu items. An example is provided below.

```
<android.support.v4.widget.DrawerLayout
    xmlns:android="http://schemas.android.com/apk/res/android"
    xmlns:app="http://schemas.android.com/apk/res-auto"
    xmlns:tools="http://schemas.android.com/tools"
    android:id="@+id/drawer_layout"
    android:layout_width="match_parent"
    android:layout_height="match_parent">

    ...

    // Add your toolbar, fragment container, and navigation drawer here

</android.support.v4.widget.DrawerLayout>
```

The updated "activity_main.xml" layout file is provided below. This drawer layout widget encapsulates the material toolbar, fragment body container, and navigation drawer layout.

```xml
<android.support.v4.widget.DrawerLayout
    xmlns:android="http://schemas.android.com/apk/res/android"
    xmlns:app="http://schemas.android.com/apk/res-auto"
    xmlns:tools="http://schemas.android.com/tools"
    android:id="@+id/drawer_layout"
    android:layout_width="match_parent"
    android:layout_height="match_parent">


    <LinearLayout
        android:layout_width="match_parent"
        android:layout_height="match_parent"
        android:orientation="vertical">

        <LinearLayout
            android:id="@+id/container_toolbar"
            android:layout_width="match_parent"
            android:layout_height="wrap_content"
            android:orientation="vertical">

            <include
                android:id="@+id/toolbar"
                layout="@layout/toolbar" />
        </LinearLayout>

        <FrameLayout
            android:id="@+id/container_body"
            android:layout_width="fill_parent"
            android:layout_height="0dp"
            android:layout_weight="1"/>

    </LinearLayout>


    <fragment
        android:id="@+id/navigation_drawer"
        android:name="com.learning.android.project.DrawerFragment"
        android:layout_width="@dimen/drawer_width"
        android:layout_height="match_parent"
        android:layout_gravity="start"
        app:layout="@layout/navigation_drawer"
        tools:layout="@layout/navigation_drawer"/>

</android.support.v4.widget.DrawerLayout>
```

Step 19: Create one Fragment for Each Menu Item.

Create one fragment layout for each menu item. Create the following layout files in res → layout directory.

1. fragment_assignments.xml
2. fragment_classes.xml

3. fragment_tests.xml
4. fragment_grades.xml
5. fragments_notifications.xml
6. fragments_home.xml

Create a "fragments" directory inside your "com.learning.android.project" package. Create the following listed fragment classes inside the "com.learning.android.project.fragments" package.

1. AssignmentsFragment.java
2. ClassesFragment.java
3. GradesFragment.java
4. NotificationsFragment.java
5. TestsFragment.java
6. HomeFragment.java

Each fragment class inflates its corresponding layout files. The complete "fragment_assignments.xml" file is provided below.

```xml
<RelativeLayout xmlns:android=
    "http://schemas.android.com/apk/res/android"
    xmlns:tools="http://schemas.android.com/tools"
    android:layout_width="match_parent"
    android:layout_height="match_parent"
    android:orientation="vertical"
    tools:context="com.learning.android.materialdrawer.
                fragments.AssignmentsFragment">

    <TextView
        android:id="@+id/label"
        android:layout_alignParentTop="true"
        android:layout_marginTop="100dp"
        android:layout_width="fill_parent"
        android:layout_height="wrap_content"
        android:gravity="center_horizontal"
        android:textSize="45dp"
        android:text="Assignments"
        android:textStyle="bold"/>

    <TextView
        android:layout_below="@id/label"
        android:layout_centerInParent="true"
        android:layout_width="fill_parent"
        android:layout_height="wrap_content"
        android:textSize="12dp"
        android:layout_marginTop="10dp"
        android:gravity="center_horizontal"
        android:text="Assignment 1: Android Material Design" />

</RelativeLayout>
```

The corresponding AssignmentsFragment.java class code is provided below. This fragment class inflates the previously created "fragment_assignments.xml" file.

```java
package com.learning.android.project.fragments;
```

```
import android.app.Activity;
import android.os.Bundle;
import android.support.v4.app.Fragment;
import android.view.LayoutInflater;
import android.view.View;
import android.view.ViewGroup;

import com.learning.android.project.R;

// AssignmentsFragment.java
public class AssignmentsFragment extends Fragment {

    public AssignmentsFragment() {
        // Required empty public constructor
    }

    @Override
    public void onCreate(Bundle savedInstanceState) {
        super.onCreate(savedInstanceState);
    }

    @Override
    public View onCreateView(LayoutInflater inflater,
            ViewGroup container,
            Bundle savedInstanceState) {

        // Inflate the layout for this fragment
        View rootView = inflater.inflate(
            R.layout.fragment_assignments, container, false);

        return rootView;
    }

    @Override
    public void onAttach(Activity activity) {
        super.onAttach(activity);
    }

    @Override
    public void onDetach() {
        super.onDetach();
    }
}
```

Similarly, create other fragment layouts and their corresponding fragment classes.

Step 20: Update Main Activity Class to Display Fragment Body

Update the `MainActivity.java` class. This class implements the
`FragmentDrawerListener.java` class. An example code is provided below.

```
public class MainActivity extends AppCompatActivity implements
        DrawerFragment.FragmentDrawerListener {
    ...
}
```

The complete `MainActivity.java` class code is provided below.

```java
package com.learning.android.project;

import android.support.v4.app.Fragment;
import android.support.v4.app.FragmentManager;
import android.support.v4.app.FragmentTransaction;
import android.support.v4.widget.DrawerLayout;
import android.os.Bundle;
import android.support.v7.app.AppCompatActivity;
import android.support.v7.widget.Toolbar;
import android.view.Menu;
import android.view.MenuItem;
import android.view.View;

import com.learning.android.project.fragments.AssignmentsFragment;
import com.learning.android.project.fragments.ClassesFragment;
import com.learning.android.project.fragments.GradesFragment;
import com.learning.android.project.fragments.HomeFragment;
import com.learning.android.project.fragments.NotificationsFragment;
import com.learning.android.project.fragments.TestsFragment;

// MainActivity.java
public class MainActivity extends AppCompatActivity implements
        DrawerFragment.FragmentDrawerListener {

    @Override
    protected void onCreate(Bundle savedInstanceState) {
        super.onCreate(savedInstanceState);
        setContentView(R.layout.activity_main);

        Toolbar toolbar = (Toolbar) findViewById(R.id.toolbar);
        setSupportActionBar(toolbar);
        getSupportActionBar().setDisplayShowHomeEnabled(true);

        DrawerFragment drawerFragment = (DrawerFragment)
                getSupportFragmentManager().
                findFragmentById(R.id.navigation_drawer);

        drawerFragment.setUp(R.id.navigation_drawer, (DrawerLayout)
            findViewById(R.id.drawer_layout), toolbar);

        // Set the drawer listener
        drawerFragment.setDrawerListener(this);
    }

    @Override
    public void onDrawerItemSelected(View view, int position) {
        // Displays selected fragment
        displayFragmentView(position);
    }

    // User can view the selected fragment in its container
    private void displayFragmentView(int position) {
        Fragment fragment = null;
        String title = getString(R.string.app_name);
        switch (position) {
```

```
            case 0:
                fragment = new HomeFragment();
                title = getString(R.string.nav_item_home);
                break;
            case 1:
                fragment = new ClassesFragment();
                title = getString(R.string.nav_item_classes);
                break;
            case 2:
                fragment = new AssignmentsFragment();
                title = getString(R.string.nav_item_assignments);
                break;
            case 3:
                fragment = new TestsFragment();
                title = getString(R.string.nav_item_tests);
                break;
            case 4:
                fragment = new GradesFragment();
                title = getString(R.string.nav_item_grades);
                break;
            case 5:
                fragment = new NotificationsFragment();
                title = getString(R.string.nav_item_notifications);
                break;
            default:
                break;
        }

        if (fragment != null) {
            FragmentManager fragmentManager =
                            getSupportFragmentManager();
            FragmentTransaction fragmentTransaction =
            fragmentManager.beginTransaction();
            fragmentTransaction.replace(R.id.container_body, fragment);
            fragmentTransaction.commit();

            // set the toolbar title
            getSupportActionBar().setTitle(title);
        }
    }

    @Override
    public boolean onCreateOptionsMenu(Menu menu) {
        /* Inflate the menu; this adds items to the action bar if it is
              present. */
        getMenuInflater().inflate(R.menu.menu_main, menu);
        return true;
    }

    @Override
    public boolean onOptionsItemSelected(MenuItem item) {
        // Handle action bar item clicks here. The action bar will
        // automatically handle clicks on the Home/Up button, so long
        // as you specify a parent activity in AndroidManifest.xml.
        int id = item.getItemId();

        //noinspection SimplifiableIfStatement
```

```
        if (id == R.id.action_settings) {
            return true;
        }

        return super.onOptionsItemSelected(item);
    }
}
```

Step 21: Check Your Project Structure in Android Studio

Verify your project files and package structure in Android studio. Figure 8-7 shows the completed project structure.

Figure 8-7: Project structure with files and packages

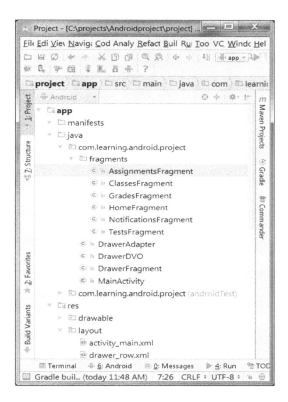
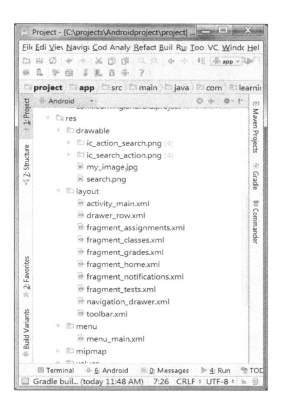

Step 22: Test the Application

Run the application and view the navigation drawer. Figure 8-8 show various test scenarios.

Figure 8-8: Material navigation drawer

1. Click on hamburger icon → navigation drawer will be dsiplayed with menu items
2. Click on Assignments → Assignments will displayed
3. Click on Classes → Classes will be displayed.

Similarly, test the other scenarios. Figure 8-9 shows the assignments and classes.

Figure 8-9: Assignment and classes fragment

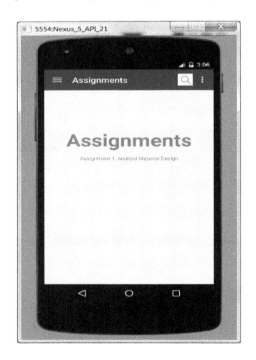

Project Tutorial: Develop a Practice Project

Step 23: Add a New Menu and Menu Items to the Toolbar

Update the "menu_main.xml" file with new items. Open res → menu → menu_main.xml file. Add the following menu items.

```
<item
    android:id="@+id/item1"
    android:orderInCategory="100"
    android:title="item 1"
    app:showAsAction="never" />

<item
    android:id="@+id/item2"
    android:orderInCategory="100"
    android:title="item 2"
    app:showAsAction="never" />

<item
    android:id="@+id/item3"
    android:orderInCategory="100"
    android:title="item 3"
    app:showAsAction="never" />
```

Update the following methods to the `MainActivity.java` file.

```
@Override
public boolean onCreateOptionsMenu(Menu menu) {
    getMenuInflater().inflate(R.menu.menu_main, menu);
    return true;
}


@Override
public boolean onOptionsItemSelected(MenuItem item) {
    return MenuChoice(item);
}

private boolean MenuChoice(MenuItem item) {
    int id = item.getItemId();
    if (id == R.id.action_settings) {
        Toast.makeText(this, "You clicked on Settings",
                Toast.LENGTH_LONG).show();
        return true;
    }

    if (id == R.id.item1) {
        Toast.makeText(this, "You clicked on Item 1",
                Toast.LENGTH_LONG).show();
        return true;
    }

    if (id == R.id.item2) {
        Toast.makeText(this, "You clicked on Item 2",
            Toast.LENGTH_LONG).show();
            return true;
    }
```

```
if (id == R.id.item3) {
    Toast.makeText(this, "You clicked on Item 3",
        Toast.LENGTH_LONG).show();
    return true;
}

return false;
}
```

Step 24: Test the Application

Follow the below provided step-by-step instructions.

1. Click on menu icon
2. Menu will be displayed with items (Refer to Figure 8-10)
3. Click on item 1 → User can view the message as shown in Figure 8-10

Figure 8-10: Assignment fragment

References

The below given documents and web links are referenced in this book.

Android studio and SDK downloads - http://developer.android.com/sdk/index.html

Android material design guidelines
http://developer.android.com/training/material/index.html

Android activity life cycle
http://developer.android.com/reference/android/app/Activity.html

Fragment life cycle
http://developer.android.com/reference/android/app/Fragment.html

SQLite database
http://developer.android.com/reference/android/database/sqlite/package-summary.html

Spring Android - http://projects.spring.io/spring-android/

Green robot event bus
https://github.com/greenrobot/EventBus/blob/master/HOWTO.md

Realm IO for Android - https://realm.io/docs/java/latest/

Android shared preferences object
http://developer.android.com/reference/android/content/SharedPreferences.Editor.html

JDK File IO - https://docs.oracle.com/javase/tutorial/essential/io/fileio.html

Material notifications - http://developer.android.com/design/patterns/notifications.html

Material navigation drawer specifications
https://www.google.com/design/spec/patterns/navigation-drawer.html

Material cards and recycler views - http://developer.android.com/training/material/lists-cards.html

Animated vector drawables
https://developer.android.com/reference/android/graphics/drawable/AnimatedVectorDrawable.html

Working with animated vector drawables
http://developer.android.com/training/material/drawables.html

Layout manager or view groups
http://developer.android.com/guide/topics/ui/declaring-layout.html

Input controls or views
http://developer.android.com/guide/topics/ui/controls.html

Application manifest file guidelines

http://developer.android.com/guide/topics/manifest/manifest-intro.html

Working with menus and menu items
http://developer.android.com/guide/topics/ui/menus.html

Working with Action bar
http://developer.android.com/guide/topics/ui/actionbar.html

Android support libraries
http://developer.android.com/tools/support-library/index.html

Android build process
http://developer.android.com/sdk/installing/studio-build.html

Index